HOW THE WEST WAS WORN

5/25/12

HOW THE WEST WAS WORN

Bustles and Buckskins on the Frontier

CHRIS ENSS

TWODOT®

GUILFORD, CONNECTICUT
HELENA, MONTANA
AN IMPRINT OF THE GLOBE PEQUOT PRESS

A · T W O D O T® · B O O K

Text design: Lisa Reneson, www.twosistersdesign.com

Library of Congress Cataloging-in-Publication Data
Enss, Chris, 1961-
    How the west was worn : bustles and buckskins on the wild frontier / Chris Enss.– 1st ed.
        p. cm.
    Includes bibliographical references.
    ISBN-13: 978-0-7627-3564-8
    ISBN-10: 0-7627-3564-3
    1. Clothing and dress–West (U.S.)–History–19th century. 2. Frontier and pioneer life–West (U.S.)–Social life and customs. I. Title.
    GT617.W47E58 2005
    391'.00978'–dc22

Manufactured in the United States of America
First Edition/Second Printing

For My Brothers Rick, Scott, and Corey:
Your strength, humor, and integrity
make me proud.

CONTENTS

FOREWORD

HOW THE WEST WAS WORN IS DEFINITELY THE GENUINE ARTICLE!

This book is a stunning collection of vintage essays and rarely seen journal entries, detailing the clothes worn by settlers of the early American West.

When author Chris Enss sent me the manuscript and asked if I would write the foreword, I found it a hard collection to put down. I've always been in love with anything western. Growing up in the heyday of television westerns has given me an appreciation for silver-screen cowboys and authentic frontier buckaroos.

Not only was my youth spent watching and reading about all things western, but traveling throughout the West with my family helped give me a deeper understanding of pioneer hardships. Growing up in Florida, I was one of four children, and each summer, Dad and Mom piled us into a car and headed to the West for a six-week adventure, our Airstream trailer in tow. Our only real hardship was the lack of air-conditioning, which pales in significance to the stories you are about to read.

While traveling through the untamed wilderness of Monument Valley, we were lucky enough to visit the set of a John Wayne western being filmed by the legendary director, John Ford. It was hard not to notice the trappings and gear that the Navajos wore as we jeeped past their mud hogans to the camera set-ups. The Duke, Dobe Cary, Jeffrey Hunter, and Hank Worden galloping across the sand dunes is an image I'll always treasure.

Wayne was wearing his signature red bib-front shirt, and jeans with both a belt and suspenders. My mom had dressed me in shorts, socks, and sandals, but, luckily for me, the Duke's leather bat-wing chaps draped over my legs and feet when he knelt down for a photo op—and since I was topped off in a faded yellow "Davy Crockett" T-shirt featuring Fess Parker, it wasn't too embarrassing for an enamored six-year-old.

I always liked to dress up like a cowboy. Still do! I own over a dozen pairs of cowboy boots, several vintage pairs of chaps, spurs for every occasion, and many shirts with cowboy piping. My treasured Manuel jacket was given to me by my wife, Laura. I have too many hats to count, mostly with my favored large crown. I can mix and match western wear with the best of them, and have been fortunate to be included in so many western-related events that I'm never at a loss in finding opportunities to wear my gear.

Not only is it still fun to play at being a cowboy, it's a pleasure to read about them. That's why this book is so special. Nothing like it has been printed before, and it's a real treasury of true stories that can help us understand why and how we ended up so fascinated with our ancestors' pilgrimage.

Their journey was a tough one, and many personal belongings were left behind, out of necessity. Limited space often meant either wearing all the clothing you owned or leaving it behind. Remember they traveled by covered wagon, boat, horseback, and mule. And they walked. Many of them walked.

Because it made walking easier, pioneer women often cut several inches off the bottoms of their dresses and sewed lead shot into the hem. This kept the billowing material from blowing in the wind.

Where else can you learn that candle soot was used as eyeliner? Or that hundreds of years before cross-dressing entered our vocabulary, young men wore women's bonnets to protect their eyes from the sun's glare when no broad-brimmed hat was available. Read all about it, and more, in this wonderful book.

The stories you will discover in *How the West Was Worn* are short and fast . . . like a gunfight. Enjoy them all and relive the American dream as you follow our ancestors on their trek west.

Always your saddle pal,
Rob Word
Vice President of
Programming,
PAX Television Network

ACKNOWLEDGMENTS

Rounding up the information needed to create a book such as this is a long process. Without the assistance of knowledgeable historians, librarians, and archivists it would not be possible. With that in mind I would like to expression my appreciation to the staff at the National Archives Department in Washington, D.C., and the Archives Department at Sears and Roebuck Corporation in Chicago. Thank you to Ed Tyson at Searls Historical Library in Nevada County and the Nevada County librarians. All were helpful, kind, and patient and eager to lend their expertise.

I'd also like to extend my gratitude to Dakota and Sunny Livesay at *Chronicles of the Old West*. Their encouragement and their newspaper are an inspiration to me always.

Finally, thanks to the editorial staff and art department at Globe Pequot Press. They managed to transform the rough material submitted to them into a quality product of which I am very proud. Thank you Erin Turner; you are an exceptional editor and I am blessed to have worked with you.

INTRODUCTION

What a deformed thief this fashion is.
   —William Shakespeare, *Much Ado About Nothing*

Men and women have always distinguished themselves through fashion. The outfits they chose to wear reflected their performance of different jobs, as well as their roles in society. Due to a lack of availability, however, the average western pioneer did not have the luxury of choosing from a wide assortment of clothing to wear. The one or two outfits he did possess were selected to fit the harsh living and working conditions of the frontier. Soon after the discovery of gold ushered a flood of newcomers into the western United States, conventional fashion changed dramatically. Men traded dress pants and ties for Levi's jeans and bandanas. Ladies stowed away their expensive, hooped costumes and donned cheap calico and work boots. Because of such changes, an individual's role in society could no longer be determined by the garments he or she wore.

The pioneer look was mostly born out of necessity and, at first, was more functional than ornamental. A lady's billowing skirt and long flowing train were not practical for buckboard travel or frontier living. It was difficult for women to fulfill trail duties while bound in stiff whalebone waist cinchers and stubborn crinolines. Men needed to wear clothing that could withstand the rugged terrain and harsh frontier weather. Children, too, adopted less restrictive attire, allowing them the freedom to work and play alongside their immigrant parents. Fashion-wise, westward expansion equalized the masses, and within that period of changing styles, a new look emerged—a look that would enable the rest of the world to recognize a westerner on sight.

By easterners' standards, western garments were out-of-date and plain, but many settlers claimed that fashion did not matter to them. However, their diaries and journals proved just the opposite was the true. The pioneers craved the latest fashions and saved any stylish items of clothing they had for special occasions. Settlers lucky enough to get their hands on *Godey's Lady's Book* (a popular magazine of the day that featured the latest styles) read the publication from cover to cover, then copied the looks. Merchants and the ambitious wives of homesteaders sent for yards of silk, ribbons, and lace to aid western seamstresses in their fashion quest. Mothers and daughters sewed plain and durable dresses, trousers, vests, shirts, and sunbonnets by hand. But they also made decorative cuffs and collars to be worn on special occasions such as the Fourth of July and Christmas. They attached to a pioneer's plain garments with buttons.

Fashion ideas were derived not only from catalogs and magazines, but also through many legendary figures of the Old West. Famous gunfighters, military leaders, actresses, and lawmen left a lasting impression on the frontier through their actions, and in the area of style as well. Some of the most unlikely individuals helped bring about the reformation of western dress. Though varied to reflect the wearers' lives and personalities, their styles were mimicked from coast to coast.

After George Armstrong Custer—who livened up his own uniform with decorative fringe—redesigned his wife's skirts to withstand gusts of wind and look elegant while riding sidesaddle, pioneer women from Missouri to California mimicked the style. They tore apart their own dresses and skirts and remade the garments to look like Elizabeth Custer's clothing. Entertainer Lillie Langtry had the same effect when she introduced bejeweled, tight-fitting corsets worn over dresses and blouses as opposed to underneath them. Bat Masterson prompted many men to substitute their standard cowboy hats with bowlers. And Oscar Wilde's visit to the West in outfits that combined the British idea of what settlers wore with a bit of the actual everyday dress set another standard.

Cowboys created a unique western style that has been duplicated for centuries. Much of their clothing made a statement. Westerners could tell where a cowboy was from based on the shape of his boots and the size of his hat. Every item of his range uniform served a purpose, and his clothes varied according to location and a cowboy's own fancy.

Clothing among Native American people varied in both style and raw material, reflecting cultural preferences and the environmental conditions found in the different regions of the West. Their garments were frequently adorned with elaborate and colorful designs and motifs, and often were indicative of a specific tribal group and an individual's status within that group.

How the West Was Worn explores how changes in fashion ran alongside the changing western United States. From morning caps to nightclothes, homesteaders to soldiers, western inhabitants created a style that set them apart from all other citizens of the United States.

CHAPTER 1

DRESSING FOR A GOLD RUSH

CLOTHES MAKE THE MAN

Like many of the young men seeking their futures in the western frontier, Canton Wells, a gangly youth dressed in a patchwork of hand me down clothes, found the dream of prosperity elusive. Drifting from town to town he made his way through the west by hiring on to the worst of jobs. The further he traveled the more bleak his prospects seemed. In the winter of 1873 Canton found himself in Flatwater, Iowa. The only gainful employment available was that of a swamper at the Bloated Goat Saloon, run by the Infamous "Boss" Buckland, a noted swindler, con man and local politician. Just when Canton thought his plight could get no worse, on March 11th fire broke out in the hotel where he had a small room that contained all of his meager belongings. All night long Canton, along with the rest of the towne folk, fought the inferno but by morning's first light a pile of ash and cinders was all that was left of the town's cheapest hotel. Everything he had worked for over the last seven years had been destroyed in one night. Even the clothes he was wearing were tattered and singed beyond repair.

With little more than a week's worth of wages in his ragged jeans he entered River City Junction Trade Company where he was greeted by the store's proprietor. In reply to Canton's request

SEARLS LIBRARY, NEVADA COUNTY

The well-dressed man of the Eastern drawing room was rarely seen in the West, where rougher attire was required. Clothes, at that time, certainly made the man.

for some clothes the store owner asked what seemed to be an unusual question. "What do you want to be?" the man asked. Noticing Canton's puzzled expression the owner explained, "A man's station is first announced to the folks around him by the clothing he chooses to wear." The two men talked for over an hour about the differences of practical and professional, and of formal and stylish. Canton purchased three new light calico shirts, two pair of trousers, a trimmed notched lapel vest, a herringbone suit coat, a narrow tie tac, suspenders, socks, a pair of sable tip shoes and a derby hat. To his surprise he had found that River City Junction's prices were so reasonable that he still had enough money in his pocket to get a good cleaning up at the barbershop and a fine dinner at Ma Cooms' Restaurant.

While at dinner a stately silver haired gentleman asked to share his table. The gentleman was none other than John R. Waddell, Sr., founder of Waddell Land and Cattle Company. Before the after dinner brandy and cigars had even been brought to the table Canton had secured the position of Territorial Agent, with a generous salary and expense account. Mr. Waddell was heard to say, "I can size a man up just by looking at him. And I can see that you are a man of great potential."

Within a month Canton had contracted with the Army to supply it with beef (with the help of a hand styled fur felt hat with

HOW THE WEST WAS WORN

the cavalry pinch by River Junction) and been put in charge of acquisitions for the Waddell Land and Cattle Company. By fall he defeated Boss Buckland by a landslide in the election for mayor of the now prospering city of Flatwater and had become the most influential person in the Indian Territories. Never forgetting that it was River City Junction Trade Company that helped to guide him on his road to prosperity when he was so lost and he is still a loyal customer and friend to this day."

—Advertisement from the McGregor Daily News, Iowa, March 12, 1873

NATIONAL ARCHIVES, WESTERN COLLECTION

Blue jeans and thick cotton or calico shirts, heavy boots, and a hat with a brim were the miner's uniform.

MINERS' ATTIRE

A hot blazing sun hung high over the Salt Lake Desert. Shafts of light like giant fingers thrust their beams to the far corners of the great expanse. A pair of slow-moving riders pressed forward across the terrain, their watery silhouettes bouncing off the sand. In the middle distance was the faint outline of a naked man with a canteen flung over his shoulder.

Wearing only a pair of boots and a brown faded hat, the bare-skinned man walked with great purpose across the heated ground. As the bewildered riders approached, the man adjusted his skimmer and scratched some vital organs.

"Nice hat," one of the riders said as he sidled up to him.

"No-good thieves stole my horse and my gear and left me

A miner was often recognizable from his ragged clothes and wild beard, even before his pick, shovel, and pan were noticed.

naked as a branding iron," the bare-skinned traveler said.

The two men on horseback exchanged puzzled looks. They had heard of highwaymen taking off with money and property, but never a man's clothes. "Must have been some fancy duds," the second rider commented.

"Red silk shirt, custom-fit money jacket and trousers that match," the naked man boasted. "Got them in Boston."

The riders stifled a laugh as they followed slowly behind the discouraged man. One of the men reached into his saddlebag and produced a pair of wool pants and a ragged blue shirt. Holding them up he said, "You can borrow these if you like."

The unclad wanderer stopped in his tracks and eyed the garments, thinking.

"You might as well," the second rider encouraged. "What are folks going to say if you show up in the next town like that?"

The nude sojourner responded with a smile, "How about 'there goes a man made by the Lord Almighty and not by his tailor.'"

In December of 1849 there were 53,000 miners in the gold fields, with even more gold-seekers on their way west. They came from all over the world and were dressed in unusual styles and fashions. Some were ragged emigrants hoping to hit the mother lode and replace their old, worn frocks with new ones. Some were aristocrats, dusty from their travels but neatly dressed for their arrival in the Gold Country. Throughout this period, clothing for men of the West reflected the styles and attitudes in the East; however, due to delays in communication and deliveries of goods, western styles generally lagged behind. It was not uncommon to see European miners dressed in brown or tan linen coats, vests, and trousers, wearing odd-shaped hats similar to the U.S. Mounted Dragoons forage cap. Their knee-high boots were always turned down during warm weather to allow for ventilation. Prospectors from Oregon, on a claim not far away, might be wearing broad-brimmed hats and laced up boots.

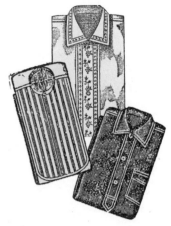

A fine calico or embroidered shirt might go west with a miner.

In the mid- to late 1800s, clothes revealed a lot about a man. How a person was attired spoke to his social standing in the community, his age, his marital status, and his geographical home. Once the massive migration west began and styles merged, it became increasingly difficult to read a man solely by the garments on his back.

Forty-niners in the gold fields invented a manner of dress that protected them from the harsh environment while maintaining a touch of their homeland's influence. It featured hats to shade their necks and faces, two pairs of shirts, and yellow-gummed leggings hanging from their belts. The bright-colored leggings helped keep the knees and trouser seams from wearing out.

Upon arriving in the Gold Country, many eastern dandies parted with their silk shirts in favor of ones made from cotton, leather, linsey-woolsey, or wool. These fabrics were chosen because they provided warmth in the winter and they quickly absorbed perspiration in the summer. White

Soft felt hats that kept off the rain and the sun with their wide brims were a very popular addition to the miner's wardrobe when they became available in the mid-1850s.

DRESSING FOR A GOLD RUSH

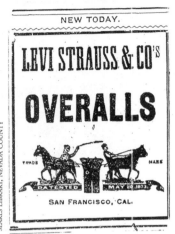

Then, as now, Levi's denim was ubiquitous throughout the west. The hardy pants were an enormous improvement over delicate gabardine in the mine fields.

shirts were worn on special occasions, and solid colors—especially red and blue—were for everyday use.

Another popular item of the time was the "fireman's shirt," a long-sleeved garment with a series of buttons down two sides of a bib. Bib-style shirts were considered a more practical design than a key-hole neck or a straight line of buttons down the middle front of a shirt because they protected the upper body better. They were originally designed for firemen and were primarily made of red wool.

No matter what the average sojourner wore in the West, most every outfit was topped off with a hat of some kind. The most predominant material used for headgear among men was straw, but in 1857 a new substance came into fashion.

Indeed, the soft felt is the only sensible hat now worn. Instead of the shiny, hard and stiff fur silk hat, so lately universal in places like San Francisco and New York. A perpetual annoyance to the owner, in his way in every conveyance and in every crowd; never protecting him from sun or rain, but keeping him anxious trying to protect it, very much in the shape and about as pleasant to the head as a section of stove-pipe would be; always getting blown off, or mashed, or weather-stained; instead of all this, we now have the broad-brimmed, flexible-bodied, easy-fitting hat, without fur on it or stiffening in it, never binding the brow or causing headache, never injured by rough handling; always in shape, if shape it might be called, which shaped has none, always shading the face from sun and sheltering it from storm; and last though not least, the prettiest hat, if beauty is associated with utility and fitness of things. This is the hat which constitutes one of the most belauded inventions of the day—one

HOW THE WEST WAS WORN

LEGENDARY TRENDSETTER

ELIZABETH "Baby Doe" TABOR

Colorado socialite Elizabeth Tabor had golden hair, blue eyes, porcelain skin, and a sense of style that rivaled that of any woman in Leadville. She arrived married to a struggling miner but dressed like she was the belle of the ball. She paraded down the main street of town wearing a sapphire-blue costume with dyed-to-match shoes. Her stunning style caught the attention not only of neighbors and storekeepers but also of millionaire Horace Tabor. Horace and Elizabeth scandalized the community by falling in love, divorcing their spouses, and marrying one another. Horace showered his new bride with jewels and the finest outfits from Boston and

COLORADO HISTORICAL SOCIETY

Paris. She wore one-of-a-kind outfits to opening nights at the opera house he had built for her.

All eyes were on the young Mrs. Tabor as Horace escorted his young bride into the theater. Her dresses were made of Damasse silk, complete with a flowing train made of brocaded satin. The material around the arms was fringed with amber beads. The look was topped off with an ermine opera cloak and muff. Pictures of the Tabors appeared in the most-read newspapers, and soon, women from San Francisco to New York copied the outfit. The only part of the costume admirers were unable to reproduce to their satisfaction was Mrs. Tabor's $90,000 diamond necklace.

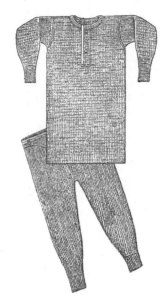

Long underwear, either in two pieces or in a single Unionsuit style, was worn by miners year-round. One hopes, rather than expects, that it was removed often for bathing.

which should universally supplant its absurd predecessor, and be worn by all classes, clergyman included.
—The Daily Alta California, *January 24, 1857*

Among the most popular pants worn by men living in the Old West were Hercules Overalls. Made from full nine-ounce York denim, they were more often than not held in place by a pair of elastic suspenders. Before 1873 the majority of britches was made from wool, sturdy canvas, or corduroy, and had an interwoven plaid design. Oregon City Woolen Mills was noted for making the finest trousers west of the Mississippi. In 1868 a single pair of Woolen Mills Hercules Overalls cost $12.

A dry goods dealer in San Francisco named Levi Strauss entered the clothing business in 1870, introducing a brand of blue denim work pants he believed was superior to any other on the market. Strauss's trousers had back pockets and rivets along the seams to provide added strength. He began mass marketing the product in 1873, but the pants did not become a big seller until seventeen years later.

At first many California transplants considered the denim pants to be "poor man's wear," solely for use by pilgrim farmers. In 1890, however, Strauss introduced a pair of "shrink to fit" jeans with straight legs. Those "Levi's" as they would later be called, made the marketer a fortune and his pants a household name.

Under the typical miners' overalls and fireman's shirt was a pair of long-handled underwear. Usually red in color, the garment was made of cotton, wool-flannel, silk, or a combination of those materials. The drawers had three or four buttons and a tie-string to hold them in place; some had tie-

HOW THE WEST WAS WORN

strings near the ankles, while others had knitted elastic gatherings at the bottom. Mail-order merchandisers like Montgomery Ward and Company and Sears, Roebuck and Company frequently advertised the "scarlet knit drawers" and "matching undershirts" in their catalogs. The underwear came in a variety of weights and cost from 45 cents to $1.25.

Some prospectors preferred to wear nightshirts under their clothes. The all-purpose covering extended to the knees and had a dual role of an undergarment and sleepwear. Those who wore long-handled underwear referred to nightshirt wearers as men who liked to sleep "dressed as cocky as the king of spades."

After their hats the most important item of clothing for miners was their footwear. Miners typically wore Hessian boots, a style derived from the boots worn by Hessian soldiers during the American Revolution. The under-the-knee boot had a square toe and moderate heel. Rounded leather flaps at the tops of some styles were used to protect a prospector's knees while kneeling. Pant legs were tucked into the boots. Elastic-sided ankle-high boots with cloth tops were preferred for special occasions. Acquiring such luxuries as formal footwear was difficult in the remote mining camps that dotted the West. In fact, the more hopeful gold seekers poured into the country, the more difficult it was to come by even the most common of items.

The summer of 1849 saw no less then 549 sea-going vessels in the port of San Francisco. In the month of August, 400

Good shoes or boots were critical for the comfort of the miner, but were also a hard-to-get luxury during much of the gold-rush period.

Men's watches graced miners' pockets as much as they did merchants and Eastern dandies. Frequently, they would be decorated with a watch fob made from hair from a far-away loved one.

large ships were idly swinging at anchor, destitute of crews; for their sailors had deserted, swimming ashore and escaping to the gold mines. 35,000 men came by sea, and 42,000 by land, during the year. The Asian coasts, Australia, South American and Africa, all contributed a melting pot of individuals that thronged the roads to the placers.

—The California Chronicle, *October 5, 1852*

Before setting off to the hills in search of gold, eager prospectors loaded up on the limited supplies available at busy mercantiles, purchasing bedding, picks, shovels, food, and an outfit of work-clothes. Shoulder-puffed sleeved shirts and black dress pants made from expensive fabric were traded for cotton shirts, denim britches, felt hats, and Hessian boots. Smaller items used to accessorize the look were also bought.

Until the late 1800s belts were not commonly used in the West. Suspenders held a man's pants in place and were made of sturdy cloth or woven tape. The ends of suspender straps were leather and contained buttonholes that attached to buttons on the trousers. Miners who struck it rich would often mount a small gold nugget on a stickpin and attach it to their suspenders.

Watches of the time were pocket-watch-style only. Usually they were wound with a key, rather than a stem-wind type and were most generally made of silver. If a vest was not worn, the watch was carried in a cloth or leather bag buttoned on the inside of the pants waistband. In 1881 Levi Strauss put a watch pocket on the front of his jeans, thereby doing away with the watch bag. Miners would wear metal chains, braided leather, or the braided hair of far-away loved ones affixed to the watches.

HOW THE WEST WAS WORN

Poor eyesight was considered a sign of old age and weakness, so it was rare to see anyone wearing glasses in the mid-1800s in the Old West. Glasses were also quite expensive, so many people were simply forced to live with vision problems. Those who could afford to improve their eyesight and face possible criticism from peers purchased ready-made, wire eyeglasses with octagonal frames.

No prospector's look was complete without a scarf or bandana. Often bright in color, the scarves were used to mop perspiration from sweaty brows and could be pulled up over the nose in cold weather. Westerners would also tie the material over their hats to hold them in place during strong windstorms.

Miners generally wore the one or two outfits of clothing they possessed until they became threadbare. Only after they exhausted their efforts at patching holes and repairing ripped seams did they purchase new garments. Prices in emporiums around mining camps were extremely high and clothing was no exception.

In 1849 Barnes Store, on the North Fork of the American River outside of Sacramento, posted the following prices for an outfit of clothes:

Socks $3.00 a pair
Denim Trousers $7.00 a pair
Shirts $4.00 each
Cotton Handkerchiefs 50 cents each

The currency of the time was almost exclusively gold. At the height of the Rush, gold was going for $16 an ounce. Miners who had yet to find any flakes at all, and could not

Eyeglasses were a rarity in the mid-1800s, but they were available for those who needed them.

afford to pay inflated mercantile prices for a new pair of britches, could wait and buy clothing from traveling peddlers, or from small temporary stores housed in a tent or under a lean-to and called "slop shops." The merchandise was limited and offered at cut-rate prices. Many slop shop owners were suspected of having stolen their inventory from merchants in San Francisco, or from supply wagon trains filled with goods making their way from the East.

Finally, the way a man wore his hair was an important part of the overall look of a miner. Most hair was parted either in the middle or on the side and was generally kept no shorter than the bottom of the earlobe. Uncooperative hair was slicked down with a perfumed oil or wagon-wheel grease.

From the tops of their heads to the bottoms of their feet, gold-field residents had a unique, rustic style of dress that distinguished them from all other western emigrants. Forty-niner Barton Bailey made note of the manner of a miner's wardrobe in a poem he published more than 150 years ago:

His trousers are quite ragged and his gray shirt torn and frayed, he wouldn't draw attention with merely the clothes upon his frame. Shifting through the dirt and gravel working his small claim, 'tis finding riches not sporting linen britches that will bring pride to his name.
—Daily Alta California, *May 12, 1854*

CHAPTER 2

CIVILIZED STYLE IN THE WILD

A COAT FOR DALE

In the days of log houses, the spinning wheel and the loom, Grandfather had gone on a long trek across the plains to the gold fields of California. Grandmother was left alone to care for their little family.

In the long winter of 1855, the snow lay deep on the prairie. For many weeks the sun shone brightly around the little cabin without a trace of melting snow. It was bitterly cold and Dale, the eldest child, badly needed a new coat.

Grandmother rose very early and began her weaving. By night she had woven enough cloth to make Dale a coat. When the evening meal was over, Grandmother cut out the cloth and began her sewing. Elizabeth, the eldest daughter, sat by her and threaded her needles. The work was done by candlelight, and as the hours passed the candles burned out.

Undismayed, Grandmother continued her sewing by the flickering flames of the logs in the fireplace. Day was breaking in the east when the coat was finished. Grandmother was very, very tired—but proud and happy in the assurance that her eldest son had a warm coat.

The daughter, Elizabeth, was my mother.

—*Emma Brawner,* Fremont Times,
Nebraska, 1956

WOMEN'S WEAR

A magnificent palomino carried its rider past a regiment of soldiers marching toward their quarters at Fort Phil Kearny, a rugged Wyoming outpost. The soldiers' heads turned to watch as the curious rider sauntered up the dusty thoroughfare to the post mercantile. The figure in the saddle pushed back a wolf fur hat and squinted into the brilliant white light of the noonday sun overhead. On close inspection one could see the person on horseback was a woman, but from a distance she could have been mistaken for a man. She was adorned in a wolf-skin outfit, and the wolves' tails on the garment hung so low they skidded across the ground. She wore knee-high boots over the legs of her ankle-length leather bloomers, and the sides of the boots were accentuated with a bouquet of wolf tails. Cavalry troops in Annie Blanche's path broke from their duties to watch the unconventionally dressed woman ride by.

Annie's face wore the expression of a patience that comes from long-endured hardship. She was aware of the many eyes following her, and she smoothed down a patch of unruly fur on her coat lapel.

Thirteen dogs trailed close behind her, adding a further touch of eccentricity to her overall look.

"Why all the dogs?" a perplexed recruit shouted out to her.

"One for each stripe in the American flag," she answered proudly.

General Marcus Thines, a distinguished military leader, stepped out of the officers' quarters just as Annie rode by. He watched her remove her primitive hat and drag her hand through her rough brown hair. "What do we have here?" the general asked the lieutenants on either side of him. "Savage, renegade, woman . . . or all of the above?"

Annie forced her hat back down on her out-of-control mane and dismounted, seemingly unaffected by the inquisitive stares and snide remarks left in her wake. She proudly headed toward the entrance of the store, confident that her fashion sense, if never duplicated, would certainly never be forgotten.

In the 1850s popular opinion was that a woman's place was in the home. Those like Annie Blanche who ventured outside those confines not only distinguished themselves by breaking with traditional roles but also with conventional manners of dress. A woman's clothing in that time was a powerful statement of who she was and to whom she was related.

Married women who wore expensive garments made from the finest silks and satins proved that their husbands

Sitting for a portrait in the nineteenth century was a momentous occaision that required a family's "Sunday best."

The ruffles, lace, and length of the most fashionable women's dresses made them cumbersome, impractical, and dangerous in the West—but fashion was still highly sought after by the settlers who saw Godey's Lady's Book *when it appeared in western outposts.*

were not just good providers but able to afford the cost of servants to attend to their wives. Society looked upon the wives dressed in muslin, tulle, lace, and organza as reflections of their husband's economic status.

The basic outfit for nineteenth-century women living in towns and cities was a hoop skirt, blouse, and bodice. Creators of the hoop skirt were granted a patent in 1856, but crude versions of the undergarment had been in use for more

HOW THE WEST WAS WORN

than ten years. Hoop skirts came in two styles: the caged crinoline and the hoop petticoat. Store-bought hoop skirts were often made from either narrow steel or stiff wire. Homemade hoops were fashioned from pieces of brass tubing or piano wire. The crinoline was a dome, funnel, or pyramid-shaped understructure made of whalebone or spring hoops used to distend or widen skirts to as large as eighteen feet in circumference.

Formal visiting dresses such as this Asian-inspired get-up would have been rare in the West—but possible for the wife of a miner or merchant who had struck it rich.

CIVILIZED STYLE IN THE WILD

Leg-o-mutton sleeves required yards of fabric to create.

Women's blouses were most often fashioned for the affluent and combined expensive materials with intricate handwork. They were available in three sleeve styles: leg-o-mutton, pagoda, and bell. The most common was the bell. This sleeve was straight and loose to the elbow, where it widened and ended just above the wrist with a soft curve.

The favorite materials for everyday wear were linen, wool, and cotton. Lace dresses were popular for formal occasions, and most typically had tight bodices and long flounced skirts. In 1862 a new dress style was introduced to eastern socialites, and within a year, the Cossack gown became the evening gown of choice, not only in Boston but in San Francisco as well.

It would seem as if the long, slim effects due to the desire to appear sylph-like have had their day, as everybody is now discussing the new Russian blouse dresses, and it is safe to say that within four weeks every woman who can compass the result will appear in a Cossack gown.

The distinguishing trait about them is a plain skirt with scant trimming and a blouse with the skirts quite long enough to come under the head of a double skirt belted in. Some of the blouse skirts reach quite to the knees and others not so far. The blouse is always open on the left side from top to bottom, and is fastened by buttons and buttonholes and by a straight, round belt with one large or two small buckles.

The blouse has this double value, as it is just the thing for a slender young figure and looks equally well on a plump one. There is a snug lining fitted like a corset cover, which is necessary.

Otherwise the blouse would "hitch." The sleeves are rather full and wrinkled at the top and plain toward the bottom.

Dresses are seen now in which there seems a determined attempt to revive the old double skirt, and these blouses come somewhat under the same head. Double skirts are not graceful, like the plain skirts, with their unbroken lines.

—Sacramento Bee, *California, June 4, 1862*

The princess dress was another popular gown in the 1860s. It was a floor-length, one-piece dress with a tight bodice and hoop skirt. The overskirt was attached to the bodice and draped up at the back of the waist. It was sometimes left unbuttoned from the waist down to reveal a pretty underskirt.

Contrary to popular opinion, not all women in isolated mining camps attended balls wearing calico dresses and old boots. There are many accounts of elaborate formal toilettes being worn in such remote Gold Rush settlements as Eureka and Downieville. When Mrs. Thomas McAlester of Grass Valley, California, attended an affair wearing a purple gown, the sheriff's wife was so taken by the garment that she contributed an article to the local newspaper describing the item:

It was a smart gown made of liberty satin. The skirt was quite full and the waist draped in folds about the figure and had cap pieces and epaulets over puffed sleeves, while a spray of purple orchids were gracefully arranged across the front of the waist.

—Grass Valley Union, *California, 1865*

SEARS AND ROEBUCK COMPANY

Servicable black skirts weighted at the bottom to prevent them billowing in stiff prairie breezes were a staple of the western woman's wardrobe.

Evening clothes worn by young or newly married women were much different from those worn by married women of middle age or widows. Younger women preferred to wear light, flowing garments made in white or pastel colors. Older women chose darker, more subdued items of clothing.

Everyday wear for women throughout the early West generally consisted of cotton, wool, or linen dresses or skirts protected by an apron. Skirts of the 1850s were simply large pieces of fabric cut into rectangles. Some had inseam pockets, while some had openings in the seams with separate pockets worn underneath. Workaday skirts and dresses were usually absent of any trim around the hem. If a woman insisted on wearing a hoop with her skirt or dress, the length of the garment measured at least 4 feet wider than the hoop. Dressy skirts, including those worn for dancing, were 2 inches from the ground. Skirts for working could be as high as 6 inches.

Most clothing for miners and their families were homemade. Women sewed endlessly, making and mending garments for themselves and for all the members of their family. The clothing they made reflected the conditions of climate, weather, and income. Woven fabrics were available at general stores and many women purchased what they could afford. Otherwise, they spun or wove most of the material needed for the clothes. The fabric was then dyed using plant leaves, stems and blossoms of wood and meadow flowers, roots, barks, nut-hulls, tree galls, berries, and fruit pits and skins. Sewing patterns were unheard of until the late 1880s; instead, clothes were cut from homemade patterns, and occasionally, old garments were disassembled into pieces and used as patterns.

Women married to prospectors lucky enough to hit the mother lode dressed in more ornate styles, but like those struggling to make ends meet, still took into account how to keep clothes clean. Caring for clothing, regardless of whether the item was homemade or store-bought, required work and time. In 1867 a two-piece dress of white cotton with a printed background became popular due to its easy care and was sold in stores, then duplicated by seamstresses throughout the West. The garment was known as the "wash dress" because it could be laundered easily. Women from all socioeconomic backgrounds wore "wash dresses."

Whether wearing a "wash dress" or Cossack gown, however, women accentuated their wardrobe with jewelry. Ivory or pearl brooches fastened to the collar at the neckline were frequently worn. Lockets could be worn on a chain or ribbon, and only earrings with wire hooks were considered fashionable. In mining communities these items were made from gold nuggets and could be worn anytime. Semiprecious stones such as garnets were worn strictly at night.

Classic replicas of Greek and Roman bracelets, tiaras, and rings were among the most fashionable jewelry of the time. Rings of this style had a tendency to hold fast to a woman's finger, leaving her to struggle with its removal during pregnancy or weight-gain. One such Arizona woman appealed to a jeweler to help remove a tight-fitting Greek band:

> *"Will you please saw this ring off my finger?" It was an old woman who made this request of an expert jeweler, and as the goldsmith took the wrinkled, though fat and shapely, hand in his, it trembled violently, and a tear dropped upon the counter.*
>
> *"Excuse me," continued the old lady, "but it is my wedding ring. I have never had it off since I was married forty-*

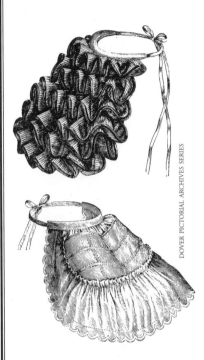

Rufffled or padded bustles were often worn beneath floor-length skirts to acheive a fashionable profile.

A wide hoop skirt might be cumbersome—and even dangerous—but it remained in fashion in spite of the efforts of dress-reform advocates such as Amelia Bloomer.

five years ago. I have refrained from having it cut, hoping that my finger might get thinner and that I could take it off without breaking it."

"And what if I can remove it without cutting?" inquired the jeweler.

"But can you?" said she, looking up in a half credulous way. "If you can do it, by all means."

HOW THE WEST WAS WORN

Then the jeweler took the swollen finger and wound it round from the top downwards in a length of flat rubber braid. The elastic cord exerted its force upon the tissues of the finger gently and gradually until the flesh seemed to be pushed down almost to the bone. The old woman's hand was then held above her head for a brief interval. Then the bandage was quickly uncorded and rewound about the member. This was repeated three times, and finally it was found upon uncovering the finger that it was small enough to admit of the ring's being removed with ease.

"I have never failed but once," said the jeweler, "and I have removed many rings from fingers even more swollen than yours. Do I charge for it? Oh, yes. I ask the same amount that I would get if the ring were left to be mended after being cut. One dollar."

"Thank you," she said.

As the old woman left the store, he turned to his bench and added: "But after all she might have done the same thing herself. It's not the work, however, I charge for; it's the 'know how.'"

—The Arizona Sentinel, Yuma, Arizona Territory, June 12, 1897

Maneuvering through the dusty streets and rough terrain of the Wild West proved women's complicated wardrobe of hoop skirts, elaborate jewelry, and long gowns impractical. A lady's traditional floor-length garments hampered her ability to move freely, and in some instances were health hazards. Many women were disfigured or killed as a result of burns suffered when their voluminous skirts caught fire without their noticing it until they were engulfed in flames. There were even accidents involving women's bulky crinolines that led to injury and sometimes death.

About 11 o'clock on Thursday night a shocking accident occurred resulting in the death of a highly respected young lady, Miss Kate Degraw. Miss Degraw, together with her two sisters, had attended a picnic a few miles out of town, in company with a young gentlemen named Ennis. Upon their return the carriage drew up to the door and the two sisters had alighted, and as the deceased was being assisted from the carriage, the horses took a sudden fright and dashed off at furious speed.

The young lady's crinoline became entangled in the steps of the carriage, and with her head and shoulders dragging upon the ground, the horses made the circuit of the village twice before the citizens could stop them. When they did so the young lady was found to be lifeless, and her remains presented a mutilated and ghastly appearance.

—Pioche News, *Nevada, July 17, 1865*

There were sanitary problems with long skirts as well. Lifting up the yards and yards of the garment's material, along with the heavy metal hoops under the skirts, was difficult. Women could not avoid dragging their clothing through the dirt and mud. An ambitious inventor from Kansas, seeking to rectify the dire situation, created a device to help ladies protect the hem of their clothes from the elements. The "instant dress elevator" was advertised for sale across the plains for the modest price of 45 cents.

You can raise your skirt while passing a muddy place and

The bloomer costume was considerably more practical than a flowing skirt for the woman daring enough to attempt a bicycle.

then let it fall, or you can keep it raised with the elevator. It keeps the skirt from filth. It can be changed from one dress to another in less than two minutes.

—Leavenworth Daily Times, *Kansas, 1874*

Ladies' heavy, cumbersome clothing was a nuisance in the home as well as in public. There was not enough room in the small kitchens of mining cabins for the cook, the cook's clothing, and the food. During working hours the hoop skirts were removed and hung on nails driven into the walls. Occasionally, the hoop skirts were stolen from argonauts' homes, only to be found later on Native American women at nearby settlements. They were fascinated with the garments, and wore them at evening dances with shawls draped over the wire.

In 1851 a voice rose up from a crowd of frustrated females and the active movement for change in women's dress began. Amelia Bloomer, an abolitionist and reformer, introduced to the public the first-ever women's trousers. The frilled pants were worn under a short skirt and were gathered about the ankles. Bloomers, as they would later be called, became the style from coast to coast. Women welcomed this turn toward comfort over convention, practicality over fashion. Men, on the other hand, were appalled at the costume, insisting the clothes threatened femininity, motherhood, and family.

It's a disgrace to see females dressed in trousers—an offense to the very fabric of civilization. I was witness to a display of "bloomers" the other day. The young woman's skirt was unusually short. It was an outrage!

—*Colorado miner Arlo Howell's journal entry, May 29, 1853*

LEGENDARY TRENDSETTER

AMELIA BLOOMER

The daughter of Dr. Hanson, of this city,
appeared in the bloomer suit at a convention
last week. It was scandalous.

—*THE SACRAMENTO BEE*, CALIFORNIA, MAY 26, 1861

Amelia Jenks Bloomer was a newspaper editor, public speaker, and proponent of women's rights and other social reform. She did not design the then-daring outfit that carries her name—a short dress that reaches below the knees with frilled Turkish-style trousers gathered in ruffles at the ankles. She *did* promote the costume, wore it herself, and watched it become a symbol of the fledgling women's movement.

Journalists in San Francisco were fascinated with the look. One reporter described the outfit he noticed on an attractive woman as a "green merino fitted over garment complete with loose, flowing trousers of pink satin, fastened at the ankle." His story included news that a dress shop owner on Clay Street not only had the bloomers on display in her window but was wearing them herself.

In yet another sighting, the city was taken quite by surprise yesterday afternoon by observing a woman in company with her male companion, crossing the lower side of the Plaza, dressed in a style a little beyond the Bloomer. She was magnificently arrayed in a black, satin skirt very short, with flowing red satin trousers, a splendid yellow crepe shawl and a silk turban a la Turque. She really looked magnificent and was followed by a large retinue of men and boys, who appeared to be highly pleased with the style.
—Daily Alta California, *September 1853*

CHAPTER 3

DRESSING FOR A ROUNDUP

THE GENUINE ARTICLE

The XIT Ranch has just established a detailed list of rules for its cowboys. Until now ranch rules were usually simple, and verbal, such as those on Charles Goodnight's ranch: no gambling, no drinking, and no fighting.

A change has been in the wind for some time now, with the ownership of the ranches switching from a boss who slept and worked with his men to today's ranches typically owned by either eastern or foreign organizations.

With cowboys not liking the change, and their feeling the rancher no longer cared about them, they have threatened to go on strike unless certain conditions are met. Their demands are simple:

"We, the undersigned cowboys of Canadian River, do by these presents agree to bind ourselves into the following obligations: First, we will not work for less than $50 per month. Second, good cooks shall also receive $50 per month. Third, anyone running an outfit shall not work for less than $75 per month. Fourth, and most important, no cowboy should be made to wear any kind of uniform that isn't the genuine article of his profession. Cowboys should be allowed to wear the shirt, pants, and leather apron of his choosing.

The uniform of the cowboy provided protection from the elements and comfort during many hours on horseback.

Sporting bib pull-over shirts of the same color does not sit well with the hires, even if it is marked with the XIT brand.
—The foreman of the XIT Ranch, Amarillo, Texas, January 31, 1888

CLOTHES FOR THE COWBOY

Ed Moultrie pushed the Stetson hat back on his head and scratched at the three-day growth of whiskers on his face. He eyed the refreshing pond water in front of him thoughtfully. He and the four other cowboys behind him had been riding the range looking for strays—with no luck—and they were hot, tired, and saddle-sore. After mopping the sweat beading his neck with a tattered bandana, he stepped off his ride. His fellow riders did the same. One by one the men shimmied out of their work boots, wool shirts, chaps, and dust-covered britches and dove head first into the inviting, murky liquid.

Ed scrubbed the dust off his body and stared up at the enormous Montana sky. As he took a deep breath and began to sink underwater, he felt something sharp along the sandy bottom. He reached down and brought up a freshly severed steer's head. He held it up for the others to see. "Aye," said one of the riders in an ominously quiet voice. "That ain't all," Ed told them. "There's more."

The cowboys found a dozen heads that had been lopped off and tossed into the stream. The men dressed and got under way quickly, the look on their faces one of dogged determination.

Riding straight west, they came to another little creek and found the evidence they sought—fresh hides with the brand "Rocking 'R'" on them.

"It be them, all right," Ed said. The gleam in his eyes was fierce now. "It'd be that damn track-laying outfit."

The men quickly found the camp and rode up slowly on the railroad workers. The foreman stood to greet them. "I can tell by your outfits you must be cowboys," he said.

Ed locked eyes with the man and without smiling said, "I want $30 for every missing steer." The foreman's fist knotted, but the grim look on Ed's face and his pointed rifle decided the issue. A check in the amount of $360 made payable to the Rocking "R" Ranch was turned over to Ed.

Cowboys were an easily recognizable group. From their Stetsons to their spurs, their wardrobe was as well known as their profession. Every item of a cowboy's clothing had a dual purpose and was decorative as well as functional.

A wide-brimmed hat keeps off rain and sun and remains key to the cowboy wardrobe even today.

Ranches might have a dress code and rules about haircuts for their cowhands.

The first men to ride the range in such rugged attire were known as the vaqueros. They were Spaniards and Mexicans who worked Mexico's missions and ranches. In California the vaqueros went by another name: Californios. Their dress was comprised of immense sombreros, broad leather belts with silver buckles, buckskin jackets, tight canvaslike horseman's trousers, half boots, and chaps. When necessary, ponchos were worn to keep out the cold and rain.

Not unlike the modern-day cowboy, the vaqueros were skilled riders who worked with wild and dangerous animals and faced many struggles on the frontier. It wasn't long before other adventurous men adopted the vaqueros' lifestyle and the cowboy was born.

Working cowboys in the Old West supplied ranches with wild cattle and horses that had been roaming the frontier. Their wardrobe was different from their Mexican counterparts but just as rugged. A cowboy's outfit revealed where he was from, how he was raised, and what he knew about the job. A fellow rider needed only to look at the style of heel on a man's boot, or the way he wore his jeans, to tell his origin. Cowboys from Nevada wore long jeans over their boots to keep out the dust and pests. Montana cowboys kept their pant legs tucked inside their boots for the same reason.

A cowboy's hat made a similar statement. Northern cowboys wore hats with a narrow brim and low crown, creased all around. Southern cowboys' hats had wide brims and high crowns.

> *Without a hat—he's just another body on the plains. Doesn't make any difference how he talks or how good he is rounding up stock. A man's hat sets him apart from the others. Boots, chaps and cowboy hats . . . nothing else matters. Without a ten-gallon hat perched on his dome he ain't a cowboy.*
>
> —*Colorado rancher Walter Bowers,*
> The Sun, *1873*

The leading maker of cowboy hats, and the man credited with their creation, was John B. Stetson. Born into a prominent haberdasher family in Orange, New Jersey, in 1830, Stetson learned the hat-making trade at an early age. In his mid-twenties he was diagnosed with consumption and advised

The style of hat worn by the cowpoke might immediately tell the viewer what part of the county he hailed from.

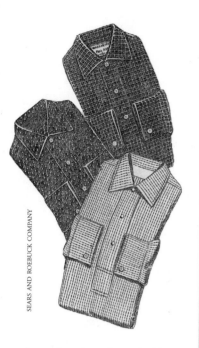

Long-sleeved, ready-made shirts were a cowboy staple.

to move to the West for his health. While traveling through the goldfields of Colorado, he created a headpiece that would protect him from the harsh weather. The result was a hat with a wide brim to keep out the elements. He also gave it a water-proof lining that could double as a water bucket. The finished hat had a 6-inch crown and a 7-inch brim.

A passing cattle driver spotted the hat on Stetson's head, along with a few extras hanging off his saddle, and offered to buy one. That first sell prompted Stetson to establish his own hat-making company, and in 1865 he began mass-producing the ten-gallon hat.

A cowboy's hat was utilitarian, used not only to protect him from the sun and rain but to carry water, fan fires, act as a feed bag or whip for his horse, and even serve as a pillow.

Bandanas—or "wipes" or "wild rags" as cowboys referred to them—were tied around their necks and were generally bright blue or red in color. They could be pulled up over a cowboy's nose when the weather turned cold or when he was riding behind herds that raised dust clouds. A bandana was long enough so that it could be draped over the cowboy hat and tied under the chin. This prevented the hat from blowing off in a windstorm and kept ears safe from frostbite during a blizzard. The bandana was even used as a towel, potholder, and bandage.

A colorful bandana provided a stark contrast to the rest of a cowboy's outfit. His shirt was typically dull in color and made of heavy cotton or wool, which was considered the best material for changing temperatures. Most shirts were pullovers with a three- or four-button front.

Long sleeves kept out the wind, cold, and sun. Sleeve garters made of elastic webbing were worn to keep the garment from catching on brush. Leather or woolen vests over the shirt provided additional warmth during chilly evenings and winter months. A fully buttoned vest helped to hold in body heat.

"The hat, the shirt, the vest. He's a cowboy."
"How do you know?"
"I can smell, can't I?"
"You can't smell cows on me."
"I can smell the look on your face, cowboy, but I love every miserable one of you. Course, you're all good for nothing, as you well know."

—Isabelle Steers (played by Thelma Ritter) to cowboy Gay Langland (played by Clark Gable) in the movie The Misfits *(1961)*

Then, as now, cowboy boots came to many styles to suit the wearer.

Cowboys preferred to wear pants of heavy wool. Their work-clothes had to be strong and durable, and wool trousers lasted the longest. California pants were the most popular style of pant. They had tight waists and loose legs and came in colors ranging from light buckskin to gray. Chapareras were worn over trousers to protect the material from brush or sharp thorns. These waist-to-ankle leather aprons—chaps, as they were more commonly known—were split up the middle and tied with leather strips at the waist and knees. Made from animal skins, the leggings were sometimes also called "hair pants." Chaps also served as good protection from rope burns, scrapes from corral poles, and even horse bites.

Boots completed a cowboy's overall look and were usually the most expensive item in his wardrobe. The average price

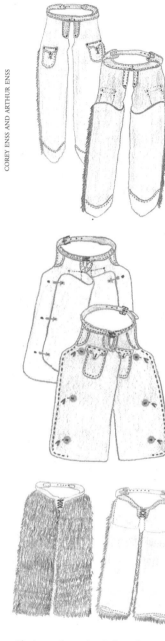

Shotgun chaps (top), batwing chaps (middle), and woolie chaps (bottom) were some of the many styles of leg protection worn by cowboys facing cacti and long days in the saddle.

for a pair of over-the-counter boots ranged from $7.00 to $15.00.

Cobbler Charles Hyer of Olathe, Kansas, is credited with creating the cowboy boot in the mid-1870s. It was patterned after the boots worn by soldiers in the Civil War. The toe was pointed so it could slip in and out of stirrups easily.

Cowboys who roped cattle on foot found that the high, thin-bottomed heels dug into the ground and helped them keep their balance. The average boot had a 17-inch-high top. This kept out dust and gravel, and protected the ankles from snakebites. Insoles were thin so riders could feel the stirrups. Boots were tight-fitting and would have been too difficult to pull on without the aid of thin leather straps on either side of the top. These pull-straps were called "mule ears."

Cowboys who preferred custom-made boots to store-bought ones had to rely on boot manufacturers on the East Coast for their shoes. The cowboy provided the boot maker with a paper tracing of his foot, his instep measurement, and $10.50 for the cost of the quality footwear.

Upon their introduction in 1875, cowboy boots were fairly plain. By 1885, however, boot makers began adding intricate leather designs and color to the footwear. One cowboy described a pair of boots he bought as having red and blue colored tops with a half-moon and star on them. Another pair of boots was described as having yellow and red fronts with a crescent and lone star inlaid in "still brighter colors."

For a time the cowboy boot was the most popular footwear in the West, but by the mid-1890s the boot had been replaced in many locations by heavy-duty shoes. Boot makers were concerned the footgear, once popular from coast to coast, was becoming obsolete.

The diminished use of boots is a matter of concern to the manufacturers of them and to the producers of heavy leather and heavy calfskins. Twenty years ago the calf boot industry was a leading one in New England. Whole towns were equipped with factories which produced calf boots exclusively.

For a decade the sale has been gradually falling off, and today it is of hardly any importance.

A few manufacturers of shoes include boots as a specialty, but the demand is too light to amount to much. When calf boots were more in vogue, manufacturers consulted the partialities of the cowboys, to whom price was a secondary consideration.

The legs were frequently corded with silk stitching. The star and crescent and other fanciful ornaments were inlaid on the legs of the boots. The high heeled boots were a striking specimen of mechanical art. The soles were inlaid with cooper, zinc and brass nails.

The cowboys no longer pay $15 for a pair of boots. They want substance instead of show. But they were not the only wearers of calf boots. Many men prefer them today though the number is growing less.

The old-fashioned stoga boots were formerly sold in large quantities. They are well obsolete. There followed a demand for a lighter more stylish article. A hip boot of finer texture was produced, about equal in appearance to the best calf boot, but this too has fallen somewhat into disuse, and the sales this season are scarcely over one-half the usual amount.

Even the farmers are using heavy shoes instead of boots, and if it becomes necessary to wear long legged boots they buy rubber.

—Kansas City News, *Missouri, 1874*

COREY ENSS AND ARTHUR ENSS

Spurs also came in a variety of styles to suit the user (if not the horse they were used upon). Here we have (from the top) two styles of Western spurs, followed by Mexican-style spurs, Cowboy spurs, and Cavalry spurs.

A well-dressed cowboy and his equally well-dressed horse demonstrate their lassoing skills.

A cowboy's footwear was not complete without a set of spurs, or "gut hooks" as they were called. Riders would file down the points on the star-shaped spur, and poke the points into the horse's sides to encourage it to run faster or turn quickly. The "pet maker," another term used for spurs, would find its way through a horse's thick, matted hair to the top of its skin.

When weather turned cold, cowhands wore an all-around duster. A similar garment was worn by Civil War soldiers. The duster was made of white canvas and reached to the ankles. Yellow oilskin slickers, called "fish skin" or saddle coats, were worn when it rained.

Cowboys covered their rough hands with leather gauntlets. Their wrists and forearms were protected from brush and rope burns with leather cuffs. The cuff originated in Texas in the 1880s, and the leather was plain, hand-carved,

LEGENDARY TRENDSETTER

BAT MASTERSON

It happened in Dodge City, Kansas. A stranger in town asked a resident where he could find Bat Masterson. A lawyer who overheard the question broke in and said, "Look for one of the most perfectly made men you ever saw, a well-dressed, good-looking fellow and when you see such a man call him 'Bat' and you have hit the bull's eye."

Masterson was known for his trim, neat style, his derby hat, tailor-made pants and jackets, and linen shirts imported from France. He was proof that being a tough lawman did not mean one had to dress like a cowhand.

Even die-hard cowboys would have abandoned their workaday garb for a dress suit like one of these for a special occasion.

or adorned with nickel studs. According to the popular slang at the time, a cowboy who was decked out in an abundance of such gear was said to be "wearing so much leather it was sweating down him like a tallow candle."

Landowners and cattle barons who owned livestock had a dress unique to their station, but not so far removed from the rugged country where they lived. Informal wear consisted of a "sack coat"—a tailored, boxy garment with ample sleeves. A cattle baron's darkly colored pants were somewhat baggy at the knees, but were long enough to reach the heels of his shoes. His shirts were made of handkerchi]ef linen and had a pleated or ruffled front. Collars were disposable, stiff standing, and made of linen bonded to paper. Ties were narrow and vests were silk and adorned with a double row of buttons. Footwear included square-toed bowed pumps, half boots, and shoes made from lace.

Whether you owned or herded cattle, how you dressed in your leisure time was just as important as how you dressed for work. Reports, such as the following, attest to the importance of a cowboy's overall look.

Terrance Lewis, a prominent cattle rancher in Durango County, was in the depth of perplexity as to his status in the affections of a certain, or, more properly speaking, a very uncertain, young woman who he had much adored. He had been so deeply in love for more than a year that he had eyes, ears, and thoughts for none other than pretty, fascinating Miss Landus.

Not wanting to express his love nor his intentions until he believed himself to be quite solvent, Terrance kept his feelings to himself —although he was certain Miss Landus

HOW THE WEST WAS WORN

could read the feelings in his eyes when they saw one another in church on Sundays.

When the day came that he should make his feelings known and propose to the fair maid who had captured his heart, he spent the better part of the afternoon preparing.

After donning his finest dress suit, it occurred to him that he would feel easier and consequently appear to better advantage in his tuxedo. At length, attired to his satisfaction, he felt he was not so bad a figure of a man after all, and that a girl might well be pleased.

Upon reaching Miss Landus's home, he was ushered into the parlor, where she was alone playing the piano. She turned to him and smiled. That was all the encouragement he needed to profess his love.

Miss Landus was taken aback. "Is it possible that you did not receive my announcement?" she asked. "What announcement?" Terrance demanded in amazement. "My engagement to Morris Bookleigh," she replied, with a happy smile.

Terrance quickly left the home without saying another word. He packed his things and set sail for Vienna the next morning, where it is said that a young beauty, impressed with his manner of dress, fell instantly in love with him. The two were married by the ship's captain once they were out to sea.

—The Colorado Sentinel,
February 15, 1892

CHAPTER 4

SONS AND DAUGHTERS OF THE TRAIL

A CHILD'S GIFT

"The most trifling gift is often the one to be valued most, and I have one that a king's ransom could not purchase," writes a gentleman who was once a teacher in a country school district.

"I had among my pupils some years ago a singularly beautiful and winsome little girl named Mary. Her parents were dead, and she had the misfortune to live with a distant relative who made the child most unhappy by his cruel treatment. His wife was even more cruel to the helpless child, who was the most obedient and submissive of children.

"They allowed her to come to school three months during the coldest winter weather. She was always thinly clad, and I fear that her little tin lunch-pail seldom contained anything better than dry bread and cold potatoes.

"I tried to be very kind to her. I hope that I was. But I had a large school of bad boys and mischievous girls who surely tried my patience, and who took up all my time, even at noon and recess hours.

"Mary was shy and sensitive, making few friends, and saying nothing when certain thoughtless and heartless girls ridiculed her shabby clothes. She had a way of twisting her

In this affluent school, a teacher poses with her well-dressed class.

thin, white fingers together and glancing around in a frightened, timid manner when she was thus taunted.

"I always went to the rescue as soon as I could, and am not at all sorry now because I boxed certain ears very smartly on Mary's account.

"The week before Christmas she fell ill. I went to see her every evening after school, and her gratitude for these visits shone forth in her eyes. I feared from the first that she would never be well again, and I think she felt so herself, and was not sorry.

"I took her a few little gifts on Christmas morning, and after I had given them to her she slipped one little thin

HOW THE WEST WAS WORN

white hand up under the pillow and said:

"'I've got a little something for you. It ain't anything hardly. I'm most ashamed to offer it; but it will do for you to remember me by, and it's all I've got to give.'

"Her little gift consisted of a small carnelian ring that could not have cost more than five cents. 'I'd like to have you keep it,' she said in a whisper. And I have kept it among the things I treasure most.

"In another hour she was raving with delirium. 'I wish, I do wish they'd stop it!' She cried. 'I wish they'd not point at my old clothes so! I hate so to put them on! I wish, I do wish I could have–new–ones–sometime!'

The young teacher in this photograph taken at a sod house school was probably not much older than the oldest children in her class, but she would have donned long skirts to take on the responsibility. Shoes were a luxury worn on special occasions and in winter for many pioneer families.

A well-dressed boy in a prosperous family would have had one of these Zouave suits.

CHILDREN'S FASHIONS

A crimson sun stained the impossible blue sky looming over a cheerless group of pioneers. The air was still and quiet as a pair of somber teamsters emptied spades of fresh earth into an open grave. The loose dirt fell on the faces of a deceased woman and her baby. Both wore such peaceful expressions that, apart from their resting place, one would have thought the pair was simply sleeping.

The small band of travelers surrounding the unfortunate souls' burial place kept their heads bowed. A plump, bespectacled minister led the westward emigrants in a prayer. The eight-year-old boy next to him stared straight ahead, fighting back a flood of tears. When he had left Independence, Missouri, with his family, he was filled with promise. The ever-expanding frontier offered many opportunities, and his father had assured him that they would take advantage of every prospect. They were on their way to Oregon to claim a piece of land and build a homestead. An outbreak of cholera had prevented that dream from coming true. The boy's father had died in Casper, Wyoming, and 28 miles later, his mother and infant sister died as well.

The weary travelers were aware the boy was now alone, and once the service ended, they spoke to one another in hushed tones about the fate of the child. Some suggested the boy be taken back East to where his family was from; others insisted he be left at the next outpost. After much discussion it was decided that a couple with nine children would see the lad safely on to Oregon. What to do with the boy after they arrived would be determined then.

The orphan retrieved some of his parents' possessions from their buckboard—he was too young to drive the team and there wasn't an extra driver to manage the vehicle, so he was forced to leave them behind. With the exception of his mother's Bible, his father's pocket watch, and an extra shirt, the boy abandoned the property and hopped aboard a Conestoga filled with children. All he owned in the world was in his hands and on his back.

The trek over the plains could be hazardous and the losses could be profound, but for those hoping to make a new life in the land eastern newspapers had claimed was filled with milk and honey, it was worth the effort. Boys and girls journeying over the plains did not commonly have many possessions or clothing. Children who lived in the 1800s generally had two outfits. Those who arrived in California as orphans might not even have that.

Like women's clothing, children's garments reflected their family's social status. In cities, fashionable parents dressed their children in the latest styles—clothing that resembled the outfits worn by adults. On Sundays and on special occasions, girls wore fancy dresses with tight bodices and boys wore formal suits. Everyday wear for these children consisted of loose-fitting skirts, sailor suits, and knickers.

In rural areas everyday outfits for boys consisted of a cotton shirt, trousers, and suspenders. Girls wore long skirts that came to their ankles, simple blouses, and long aprons or

Ruffles and dainty shoes were expected on a well-dressed young man.

A baby with wealthy parents might have fancy booties and embroidered gowns, but a less fortunate child might have to do with too-large castoffs from an older brother or sister.

pinafores over the garments. The pinafore protected clothes from stains. Because clothing of frontier children was generally passed down to younger children, and thus needed to last longer, a fabric called linsey-woolsey was used to make the most of the outfits. Some articles of clothing, such as breeches or buckskin, were made of soft leather.

General stores in remote western towns and mining camps did not stock many items of clothing. The women of the family were responsible for making outfits for all of the children who might live in a home, possibly ranging in age from six weeks to sixteen years. In rare instances where seam-stresses were available, they would be called upon to make garments for the family. Some of those women had definite ideas about the children they outfitted. A newspaper report dating back more than a century playfully describes the various thoughts on the subject:

"If I had a dozen children I would want them all boys," said Mrs. Thrifty. "Boys can take care of themselves; they are energetic, enjoyable, and it doesn't take half as much sewing to keep a family of boys along."

"Now, if I should have any choice," said Mrs. Workhard, "I should rather have my children all girls. Girls are so gentile [sic], so helpful, have so much more refinement than boys; and then it is such a pleasure to sew for them, they look so pretty in the garments made for them."

"Very well, ladies," said Mrs. Sensible, "you are both right and wrong. I believe in a mixed family—part boys, part girls. The boys influence the girls to self-reliance; the girls refine the boys by their gentleness. A boy who is brought up with sisters makes the most manly man, and the girl who

HOW THE WEST WAS WORN

is brought up with brothers makes the most womanly woman."

—Sacramento Bee, *California, July 31, 1882*

From the moment a baby was born to settlers, its clothing made a statement about its parents. All infants had diapers in common, but the way they were fastened separated the rich from the poor. Diapers were simply squares of soft linen or cotton fabric, which were folded into the proper size with each wearing. In families of modest means, the mothers typically stitched their children into the diapers after each change. More prosperous women could afford diapers made with loops and ties on the side. Most babies were generally tightly wrapped in strips of cloth and tied to a small board that supported their back. In the 1830s it was widely believed that this practice promoted good posture and the growth of strong bones.

Infants were dressed in other items of clothing as well. A less fortunate infant's wardrobe consisted of long undershirts, a bonnet or cap, and a receiving blanket of flannel. Babies from well-off families wore long dresses, which were usually white and trimmed with embroidery or lace. The excess material on infants' dresses was gathered and tied with a ribbon just below the feet. This kept the baby's body temperature up and supposedly helped to prevent colds. Babies wore dresses of varying lengths until they were five years old.

After the age of five, wealthy little girls wore hand-beaded crinoline skirts made of velvet so that when their skirts flew up as they tumbled about, the view of their undergarments would be as attractive as the rest of their garments. Boys from well-to-do backgrounds wore Zouave suits, which featured breeches

SEARS AND ROEBUCK COMPANY

Girls' dresses and hats often followed the styles favored by their mothers for their own clothes. Little girls dreamed of being old enough to let their skirts down and wear their hair up.

These simple outfits and hats reflected what was "Sunday best" for these children in Alamo, New Mexico.

and a short jacket decorated with braid. A shirt with a small collar was worn beneath the jacket. A poor girl wore knee-length calico dresses, with ruffled trousers called pantalets underneath. Young boys of modest means wore overalls or brownie suits, which were also called rompers and were strictly used for playing outdoors.

A child's footwear was the most obvious indicator of the wealth of his or her family. Children from wealthy families always wore shoes, and also wore gaiters over their shoes in the winter, in order to keep their legs warm and dry.

Because footwear was expensive, poor children went barefoot whenever the weather permitted. When they did wear shoes, boys wore heavy leather ones with thick soles, and girls wore ankle-high, laced boots. Shoes were worn to weddings, funerals, school, and church. To preserve the life of the shoe, children often carried them to each location. When the weather turned cold enough to warrant the possibility of frostbite, poor children typically stayed home from school.

Fashions that helped to combat the frigid weather, for boys and girls from all walks of life, included woolen socks and mittens. Children of wealthy families wore fur-lined capes, long woolen coats, matching leggings, fur caps, and woven wool and cotton facemasks. For boys and girls of poor families, woolen underwear and thick sweaters were their only protection from the harsh elements.

Perhaps the most important component of a child's wardrobe, however, was the way a child presented himself to adults. "Good etiquette and orderly conduct should be just as essential to any look as trousers or petticoats," remarked pioneer schoolteacher Charlotte Crabb from Tucson, Arizona, in 1887. Articles in popular newspapers throughout the West contained advice on how to teach children to behave appropriately and mannerly at all times. Crabb stated that "right actions are the key to a child's daily outfit."

Good conduct at meals is, with children, a fair criterion of good manners; and meals may be made use of, as favorable opportunities for inculcating propriety of behavior.

Children should be taught to sit down, and rise up from the table, at the same time, to wait whilst others are served, without betraying eagerness or impatience, to avoid noise and conversation, and if they are no longer confined to the nursery, to be able to see delicacies without expecting or asking to partake of them.

To know when to be quiet is more important to good

Girls wore pretty dresses and were expected to sit quietly with books or embroidery.

manners than is generally supposed. Speaking, when it interrupts reading or conversation, and the habit of contradicting others should be checked, as also, that ill-timed garrulity, so unpleasing in some children, and which, generally, springs from an undesirable self-confidence and forwardness of character.

. . . With all our care, however, we are not to expect that the manners of children will be superior to those of the persons with whom they chiefly associate; for, in nothing is it more true, that "we are all a sort of chameleons, and still take a tincture of things around us." On this account, as on

DOVER PICTORIAL ARCHIVES SERIES

Boys' outfits were more suited to stilts and other more active games.

any other, it is of importance that children should witness no vulgar habits in the nursery, and that the conversation between the nurses themselves should be guarded and correct.

But here it must be remarked that in our earnestness to render our children pleasing, and to improve their manners, care will be required that we do not rob them of their chief charm, the simplicity of childhood; for how greatly are to be preferred, even an uncouthness of behavior, and awkward shyness, to any thing of premature forwardness, formality or affection.

—Arizona Daily Star, *July 29, 1887*

LEGENDARY TRENDSETTER

ANNIE OAKLEY

Annie Oakley's ability with a gun made her famous, but she also had a glowing reputation as a seamstress. A young Annie was taught how to sew while living and working at an Ohio county home. Her teacher, Mrs. Ira Eddington, recognized her talent for knitting and stitching, and encouraged the sharpshooter to make clothing for children and the elderly.

Throughout her life, Annie Oakley made most of the garments she wore. She designed the costumes she wore in Buffalo Bill's Wild West Show, and sewed the detailed embroidery that lined the sleeves, bodice, and hem of each outfit.

The photo to the right features one of Annie's favorite outfits. This was one of the simplest styles she wore and one of the easiest to replicate. The five-gore skirt and jacket are made from the same fabric—a beige woven poplin or broadcloth. The skirt is sewn together by matching notches. The hemming and trim is applied before sewing up the back seam. The waistline is gathered as shown and sewn on to the waistband, which is doubled lengthwise. The jacket pattern consists of a front, back, and sleeve, plus neck facings that are cut from the front and back patterns. Sew shoulder seams first, apply the neck facing, then gather the sleeves and hem. Fold back facing at jacket center front and apply buttons or snaps to close.

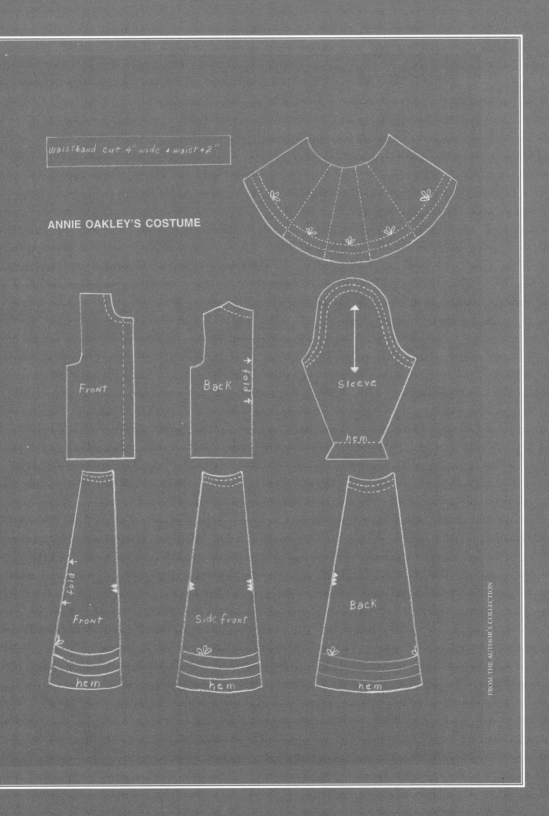

ANNIE OAKLEY'S COSTUME

CHAPTER 5

PRAIRIE STYLES

A FASHIONABLE ENCOUNTER

A hot July breeze skidded across the banks of the Green River south of Fort Bridger, Wyoming. The clear water flowed swiftly past a grove of trees, waving with the wind. The grass on both sides of the river was spangled with flowers.

Elizabeth Graves, a handsome woman in her late 40s, was decorating a tree branch hanging over the water's edge with bluebonnets. She was dressed in a green calico garment with short sleeves, lace collar and lace caplets. Her long brown hair was twisted into a bun on top of her head.

Elizabeth's husband Franklin stood nearby, looking uncomfortable. He tugged at the tie around the neck of his linen pullover shirt as he dragged a couple of chairs out of the back of the wagon and sat them under the copse of trees. He stopped to admire the placement of the chairs and adjust the pant-leg of the scratchy wool trousers he was wearing. His steady, steel blue eyes were wet from crying. Three of the Graves' children, ranging in age from five to nine, brushed by Franklin as they chased one another around the wagon. He backhanded the tears out of his eyes and smiled after his brood.

A pioneer family in the serviceable clothes that will take them west.

"I can't believe my little girl is getting married," he told his wife after a few moments contemplation.

"She's not so little," Elizabeth replied. "She's twenty. She's older than I was when we got married."

"Is that right?" Franklin shrugged.

"You don't remember?" she quipped impatiently.

"That was a hundred years and nine children ago, Lizzie," he retorted. Franklin stared out over the water then turned to Elizabeth and smiled confidently. "Ray Fosdick is a good man," he said. "He's a good worker. He'll make a good husband."

"And she'll make a good wife," Elizabeth added.

"That she will," Franklin agreed.

Elizabeth walked over to a baby's crib sitting by the wagon, reached down and picked up her nine-month-old son. Franklin strolled over to her and kissed her on the cheek and she handed him the bluebonnets.

"Why don't you finish putting these posies around," she suggested. "I've got to change your son. All we want anyone to smell at this wedding are the wild flowers." Franklin grinned, then buried his nose in the bouquet.

The Franklins' daughter, Mary, walked along the hillside overlooking the setting.

She strolled through a colorful assortment of blossoms, carefully selecting the best flowers and adding them to a bouquet she had started and had bound together with a lace ribbon. Mary looked up from her work and gazed out at the marvelous valley spread out before her. A gentle breeze blew past her and she held out her arms pretending to be caught up in the wind. The edges of her hand-sewn cape with a delicate, blue rose pattern danced over her hoopless, straight cotton skirt. Without thinking she opened her hand and the loose flowers scattered about. The wind blew the flora across the ground and over to the feet of Charles Stanton. Charles, an attractive, bespectacled man of medium height and build, bent down and retrieved the bundle. His opened vest with wide fashionable lapels revealed a soft display of ruffled material running up and down his chest. His trousers were loosely tucked into his wide-mouthed boots.

"These must belong to you," Charles said to Mary as he handed her the bouquet.

A simple, lovely muslin dress such as this one would have been laid away for safekeeping in a trunk during an overland journey by covered wagon.

Mary smiled politely. "Actually, they're for my sister," she said.

"I can help you pick more flowers if you like," Charles offered.

"Thank you," she replied, "I can manage."

Mary bent down to pick more flowers and Charles watched her closely.

"I hope I'm not intruding," he probed.

"Not at all," she said kindly.

"It sure is beautiful here," he added staring out over the valley. "You can almost see right into the future."

"And what does your future hold for you, Mister . . . ?" she inquired.

"Stanton, Charles Stanton," he told her. "In my future I see my own piece of land, my own home, my own hearth fire, the heads of my own horses looking over the gate bars for my hands to feed them."

Mary giggled a little. "You can see all that from here?" she asked playfully.

"Can't you? Miss . . . ?" Charles questioned.

"Mary Graves," she said giving a slight curtsy. "My view isn't as clear. All I see is a new world filled with exciting prospects."

"That's good enough for now," he assured her.

"Are you part of the Donner party heading out West too?" she asked.

"Yes," he nodded.

Mary stared out at the beautiful view, took a deep breath of fresh air, then said, "I heard someone say that there's no Sunday west of Independence, no law west of Dodge City, and no God west of Fort Bridger."

"Don't you believe it, Miss Graves," Charles said bend-ing down to pick a particularly breathtaking flower. He presented a delicate red bloom to her and she gave him a coquettish smile.

"I'll see you on the trail, Mr. Stanton," she promised.

"Yes, ma'am," Charles responded.

Mary pulled her blue slat bonnet hat down over her head and started down the hill. Charles watched her dis-appear into the horizon.

CLOTHING FOR THE HOMESTEADER AND EMIGRANT

The pilgrimage west was an arduous undertaking. Emigrants hurriedly loaded their wagon trains with as many personal belongings as they could, and if they were unable to make what little they had fit, it was left behind. Limited space forced many to wear all the clothing they owned on their backs. The basic outfit for a pioneer woman consisted of a gingham or calico dress, a sunbonnet, and a muslin apron. Men pioneers wore simple overalls, cotton work shirts, and caps or broad-brimmed hats.

Many who made the trek were poor, possessing only a single pair of boots or shoes, the soles of which would be worn off long before arriving at their final destination. Socks wore out as well, forcing settlers to wrap their feet in rags to protect them from the elements. When traveling through snow and ice, they wrapped their footwear in gunnysacks to keep their feet from freezing.

In preparation for the trip, women altered their dresses to make walking easier. Several inches were cut off the bottom of the skirt and lead shot was sewn into the hem to keep the billowing material from blowing in the wind. Men wore their trouser legs tucked into their boots for the same reason. Wearing them in this manner also kept out mud and reptiles. Pioneer women's dresses were worn without a hoop, and the bodice was lined with canvas for strength and warmth.

Before heading west, pioneers consulted guidebooks for advice on suitable dress for the trip, and how to best protect the body against the direct rays of the sun and sudden changes in temperature. If they acquired the necessary items listed, travelers were assured to be prepared for any possible condition.

A suitable dress for prairie traveling is of great import to health and comfort. Cotton or linen fabrics do not sufficiently protect the body against the direct rays of the sun at midday, nor against rains or sudden changes of temperature. Wool, being a non-conductor, is the best material for this mode of locomotion, and should always be adopted for the plains. The coat should be short and stout, the shirt of red or blue flannel, such as can be found in almost all the shops on the frontier: this, in warm weather, answers for an outside garment. The pants should be of thick and soft woolen material, and it is well to have them re-enforced on the inside, where they come in contact with the saddle, with soft buckskin, which makes them more durable and comfortable.

Woolen socks and stout boots, coming up well at the knees, and made large, so as to admit the pants, will be found the best for horsemen, and they guard against rattlesnake bites.

In traveling through deep snow during very cold weather

in winter, moccasins are preferable to boots or shoes, as being more pliable, and allowing a freer circulation of the blood. In crossing the Rocky Mountains in the winter, the weather being intensely cold, I wore two pairs of woolen socks, and a square piece of thick blanket sufficient to cover the feet and ankles, over which were drawn a pair of thick buckskin moccasins, and the whole enveloped in a pair of buffalo-skin boots with the hair inside, made open in the front and tied with buckskin strings. . . .

In the summer season shoes are much better for footmen than boots, as they are lighter, and do not cramp the ankles; the soles should be broad, so as to allow a square, firm tread, without distorting or pinching the feet.

The following list of articles is deemed a sufficient outfit of one man upon a three months' expedition, viz.:

2 blue or red flannel overshirts, open in front, with buttons.
2 woolen undershirts.
2 pairs thick cotton drawers.
4 pair woolen socks.
2 pairs cotton socks.
4 colored silk handkerchiefs.
2 pair stout shoes, for footmen.
1 pair boots, for horsemen.
1 pair shoes, for horsemen.
3 towels.
1 gutta percha poncho.
1 broad-brimmed hat of soft felt.
1 comb and brush.
2 tooth-brushes.

Hooped skirts, puffed sleeves, and eastern-style hats and hairdos made up "Sunday best" in western settlements.

1 pound Castile soap.

3 pounds bar soap for washing clothes.

1 belt-knife and small whet stone.

Stout linen thread, large needles, a bit of beeswax, a few buttons, paper of pins, and a thimble, all contained in a small buckskin or stout cloth bag.

The foregoing articles, with the coat and overcoat, complete the wardrobe.

—Randolph Marcy, The Prairie Traveler, *1859*

The same guidebooks warned women in wagon trains that, while traveling on the trail, they should dress plainly, avoid fancy attire, and never draw attention to themselves.

A gay dress, or finery of any sort . . . lays a woman open to the most severe misconstruction. Wear always neutral tints. . . . Above all, never wear jewelry (unless it be your watch), or flowers; they are both in excessively bad taste.
—The National Wagon Road Guide, *1858*

The average pioneer family's clothes were in a constant state of repair while on the rugged trail west. Women worked continually to keep their husband's and children's clothing mended. Homesteaders who kept journals of their travels reported seeing clothing beside the trails that was so worn, it had simply fallen off the backs of the owners. If family members passed away on the trip, their bodies were laid to rest after having been stripped first of their clothes and wrapped in loose cloths. Their garments were then passed on to the living.

Once a garment was beyond repair, many emigrants were forced to wear clothing of the opposite sex. Men whose hats wore out, or were carried away by the wind, sometimes resorted to extreme measures. Some female pioneers wrote in their journals about seeing young men wearing sunbonnets to protect their eyes from the sun's glare. Women who dressed in men's clothing out of necessity were often times mocked. Many men considered the act improper.

Supplying a family with clothing once they reached their journey's end was a daunting task. Where a family lived determined, to a great extent, where and how they obtained their clothing. City and town dwellers usually purchased ready-made items or fabrics from specialty or general stores. People in rural or remote areas were more likely to undertake the whole process themselves. Indeed the entire frontier family helped to produce cloth used for their clothing. Sheep were

SEARS AND ROEBUCK COMPANY

White muslin underwear could be just as elaborate as the clothes worn over it.

LEGENDARY TRENDSETTER

OSCAR WILDE

"Fashion is a form of ugliness so intolerable that we have to alter it every six months."

—OSCAR WILDE, 1883

When playwright Oscar Wilde made the long journey from London to California, he brought with him a flamboyant wardrobe. In 1882 he attracted large crowds of settlers in Leadville, Colorado, who were interested in seeing Wilde's velvet knicker suit and flowing bow tie. His outrageous costume was made complete with a high-crowned, large-brimmed cowboy hat and knee-high cowboy boots. Although men found his fashion sense questionable, women admired the frilly, soft-collared shirts he wore, and they made patterns of the garment so they could replicate the design for themselves.

fed and sheared by the men of the household. Wool cleaning and carding were done by young children. Spinning yarn, dyeing it over the fire, loom-weaving of homespun fabric, and the sewing of trousers, coats, and dresses were done by the women.

Western newspaper articles applauded resourceful families who provided for themselves. Some even went so far as to imply that their meager way of living ensured a happier life.

Poverty runs strongly to fun. A man is never so full of jokes as when he is reduced to one shirt, his wife and children to one set of handmade clothing and all to two potatoes. Wealth is taciturn or fretful. Stockholders would no sooner indulge in a hearty laugh than they would lend money on a second mortgage. Nature is a great believer in compensations.

Those to whom she sends wealth she saddles with lawsuits and dyspepsia. The poor never indulge in woodcock, but then they have a style of appetite that converts a number 3 mackerel into a salmon, and that is quite well.

—Tri-Weekly Alamo Express, *February 19, 1861*

When it was time to bunk down in the evenings, most emigrant men slept in their clothes or in long-handled underwear. Women changed into nightdresses. This garment was usually homemade and of long cloth flannel. It was frilled around the neck, down the front opening, and on the cuffs. Nightclothes of this time period were designed to hide the shape of the body and to prevent unmarried men from thinking immoral thoughts about unmarried ladies.

All types of clothing were in high demand in the small

towns and outposts that sprang up along the westward trails. Naïve families who had packed fine, elegant garments when they left their eastern homes found they could make a small fortune selling the items to pioneers in want. During a stopover in Salt Lake City, Utah, a wagon train made up of destitute emigrants sold every thread they could to earn funds or gain provisions to continue on to California.

Have traded four of my best bleached, feed-sack aprons for two pounds of bacon. Could have gotten three pounds if I'd included my 'tea apron.' But it was a gift from my mother back home in Kansas. I could not accept the offer.
—Nancy Witt, pioneer, 1853

CHAPTER 6

A LASTING EFFECT

REMEMBER ME

This wasn't the first time Maggie Kremer had turned her face away when Ransom Diggs bent to kiss her, but she caught the pained look on his face as he planted a light caress on her smooth cheek. All the other times she had withheld her lips for the same reason—jealousy. Not of another woman, but of his job. Ransom Diggs was Sheriff of Cold Springs, a silver mining town in Southern Arizona. His work often times took precedence over his relationship. Keeping the territory safe from desperados required round-the-clock dedication. It was for this reason, coupled with the fact the he might be gunned down in the line of duty, that kept Maggie, the town's school teacher, from accepting his proposal of marriage.

She tucked away a stray tendril of dark brown hair, and blinked away a tear. Ransom saddled his bronco. Neither of them said a word for a long while, then Maggie broke the silence.

"I don't see why you don't just let Charles Storms and his gang ride on to the next county," she said. "They'd be out of your jurisdiction then and you could stay with me."

"I can't do that," he told her as he cinched up the leather straps under his ride.

Maggie knew that was what he'd say and she loved him for it as much as she despised the notion of him riding off again.

"Will you be here when I get back?" he asked hopefully.

Maggie forced a smile. "Aren't I always?" she replied.

Ransom smiled back at her and mounted his horse. Maggie always thrilled a little when she watched him on a horse. He might be a bit awkward on the ground at times, but mounted, he was the handsomest man she knew. He was tall, with broad shoulders and had the narrow hips of a cowman. Looking down at his betrothed he adjusted the black hat on his head. She could see the little ducktail of straw-colored hair at the back of his neck. She wondered how much longer it would grow before she next saw him.

"I'll be home as quick as I can," he promised. The two stared a moment at each other. Maggie's eyes were pleading, but he wouldn't waver from his duty. She produced a dainty, lace handkerchief from her drawstring bag and stemmed the flood of tears breaking free. Ransom's face was filled with compassion. She walked over to him and laid her head on his leg and he stroked her long curls. Just before he announced that it was "time to ride" Maggie handed him her handkerchief.

"Don't forget me," she said jokingly. He raised the hanky to his nose, breathed in her scent, and fingered the fancy stitching around the hem. "Never happen," he assured her as he rode away.

The outlaw Charles Storms and his gang ambushed Sheriff Diggs and his posse in the mountains around Cochise Stronghold. Among the personal effects returned to Ransom's

intended nearly three months after he had left Cold Springs was Maggie's handkerchief. The men who found him claimed the delicate, blood-stained fabric was clutched in his hand.

—Tucson Daily News, *Arizona, 1892*

Best hats, long skirts, and three-piece suits make for a picturesque picnic scene.

ADDITIONS TO THE OVERALL LOOK

Women of the mid-1800s considered ornamental fineries like the handkerchief an easy piece of their wardrobe to part with. Men carried such items into battle, out to sea, and across the difficult terrain of the West. Often these small squares of material were sprayed with perfume. At the time, perfumes and

Perfumes were important to a lady's overall grooming.

A lady, it was often said, always wore gloves.

colognes were worn mostly by married women, and the fragrance of choice was predominately floral. The hope was that the fragrance would remind loved ones of the girl they had left behind and prompt a speedy return. Not all handkerchiefs possessing lingering bouquets inspired romantic sentiments, however:

Women beware. The perfumes which are most agreeable to the senses are not always the most helpful to the nerves. Ambergris, for instance, is positively offensive to many, yet it is said to possess a wonderful power of clearing the brain and driving away those evil spirits known as the "blues."

On the other hand attar of roses, with the suggestion of glowing suns and gorgeous eastern colors, predisposes one to tears. A faint odor of musk acts as a tonic, while civet brings drowsiness of soul, for which the best antidote is the pungent odor of Sandalwood. The fragrance of citron and aloe wood is as soothing to nervous people as far-off music.

Many perfumes, delightful in the open air, become particularly disagreeable in a close room. A whole evening can be spoiled by the presence of tuberose or lilies in a reception room. Their strong fragrance has a very bad effect. Magnolia blossoms, too, have a delightful perfume in their native grove, but woe to her who sleeps through the night with a single blossom on her pillow. There are many fragrant flowers, such as carnations, clove pink, sweetbriar and apple blossoms, that are as beneficial as they are sweet and scented.

A vivid perfume is nearly always bracing, while a subtle one is generally enervating. One may become positively intoxicated thro' inhaling the odor of the peach, almond, wild cherry and other blossoms of the same class, because

they all contain a suggestion of prussic acids.
—Free Press, *Mesa, Arizona Territory,*
July 9, 1897

Accessories to a woman's look were quite varied. In addition to lace handkerchiefs, gloves were considered a must—a lady always wore gloves. Short, kid gloves that matched a lady's outfit were preferred for day wear. With an evening dress, satin, lace, or net-work gloves that reach the bottom tip of the sleeve. Both kid gloves and those intended for evening wear were often decorated with fine embroidery. Women in rural areas wore gloves made from suede, cotton, and wool. Black and tan gloves were always in favor.

According to the magazines of the time such as *Godey's Lady's Book,* gloves were such a popular item of clothing that in 1892, more than 30,000 people in the United States made their living from the industry. It was such a growing market that the government imposed tariffs to protect wages and guard against foreign encroachments.

Since those protective duties were imposed American factories have become the most important sources of supply for the home market, and have turned out a product not only of a continually improving quality. The American glove is just as handsome and more

A parasol would be a rare sight on a Kansas homestead, but in the cities that were growing up in the West, it was a useful tool to keep a lady's skin fair.

A delicate lawn hankie could be found inside a lady's purse or reticule.

A paisley shawl was an indication of wealth, worn more for decoration than protection from the elements.

substantial than the foreign article and can be bought at a lower price than ever before.

—El Paso Daily Herald, *Texas, May 1892*

Women from all socioeconomic backgrounds added parasols and fans to their summer look. These items were not only decorative, but also functional. Parasols provided shade from the heat and were made from material such as cotton and linsey-woolsey for the more basic style, and lace and satin for the more elaborate. The average parasol was 24 inches across. Fans helped keep ladies cool as well, and often hung from the waists of their dresses.

According to an 1865 issue of *Godey's Lady's Book*, women were not considered proper ladies if they appeared in public without a shawl. A shawl was a common outer garment that was square, rather large, and usually made from wool. The shawl every woman coveted was a Paisley. It was patterned after the hand-woven Kashmir shawls from India. Paisley shawls ranged in price from $2.50 to $500.00. The less expensive Paisley shawls were available from Montgomery Ward and Company; the higher-priced version were imported from Scotland.

Authentic Paisley shawls were woven in a manner quite similar to methods used to weave tapestries, and the finest were woven with goat's fleece from Asia. But regardless of price or quality, Paisley shawls were worn more for decoration than protection from the elements. Everyday shawls that had a more utilitarian purpose were either crocheted or handmade from cotton or wool. Women who couldn't afford the fashionable Paisley shawl sometimes added fringe and beads to the edges of an everyday shawl.

HOW THE WEST WAS WORN

Ladies' handbags or purses were generally kept tucked inside the pockets of their full skirts. When they were worn outside, one could see they were small drawstring or clasp bags. Many purses were hand-crocheted out of beaded fabric. Still others, like the ones offered at fashionable stores in Denver, Colorado, were crafted from the finest material.

The little chain purse looks conventional enough, but when some fair shopper chances to find it she will be much delighted at the marvelous workmanship, as she will be later disappointed by the price.

It is made of iron, studded with stars of red gold. In the center of each star is a tiny sparkling diamond. The clasp is in the form of two crescents. The clasp is thickly studded with gleaming diamonds, and the effect is beautiful. The purse is about the size of a silver dollar. The back is fitted with a safety clasp pin. It is to be worn pinned on the left side of a lady's belt, a little below the waistline. It will cost $150.00.

—The Denver Republican, *Colorado, August 1899*

In the 1850s, outfits for both sexes were topped off with a hat. Most children and all adults wore some kind of head covering in public. The bonnet was the most common hat worn by women. Made from a wide range of material from calico and straw to velvet and silk taffeta, the brim of the sun-bonnet contained thin slats of wood or cardboard so that it stood out over the wearer's face. This provided protection from the harsh sun of the open country. All bonnets were fixed with a curtain from 2 to 14 inches in length hanging down at the back to conceal the neck from the elements as well.

Ladies typically tucked their tiny handbags into the pockets hidden in their voluminous dresses.

LEGENDARY TRENDSETTER

JAMES BUTLER HICKOK

Wild Bill Hickok was an American frontier army scout, peace officer, stagecoach driver, and gambler. He was a big man and his 6-foot frame was accentuated by the long wool jackets he frequently wore. The red sash he generally sported around his waist stood out over the dark pants and vest of his everyday wardrobe. The sash held two pistols, always pointed butt-forward beneath his coat. His giant brimmed hat was cocked on his head and his long wavy hair, parted in the middle, cascaded down his back. Many dime-novel readers tried in vain to duplicate his style, but only one could do the look justice.

Winter bonnets were traditionally black and made to match or coordinate with different dresses. They were made with buckram frames—a heavy, stiff, reinforced wire that made the hat stand out away from the face. Bonnet trimmings consisted of ribbons, lace, feathers, flowers, fringe, or braid. The hat stayed on the head with the use of hatpins and a tie under the chin.

Hats were considered a vital fashion accessory throughout the nineteenth century. Women were considered only partially dressed if they left their homes without headwear. By the early 1860s, the bonnet was slowly being replaced with wider, taller, and more elaborate hats. White organdy garden hats with sprays of flowers were the style in the East. In the West, the Hussar hat was the rage. The Hussar was a low-brimmed military hat that was redesigned for ladies and included layers of lace and tulle. Straw hats from Paris were popular from coast to coast—fancy yellow straw and appliquéd lace hats topped off many looks.

Newspaper editors in California cautioned finely dressed women with such hats not to overrate the attention they received from their fashions. They warned, "The girl who expects to win her way in life with her beauty and a grand hat alone may be disappointed."

Hats elaborately trimmed with feathers and ribbons would have been saved for city wear or Sunday best. Bonnets intended to keep off wind and sun would have been more typical on a homestead.

To win and hold admiration you must first cultivate the gifts that nature has bestowed upon you. If you have a talent for music, develop it; learn to play some instrument; for many are more charmed by music, than by handsome features or clothing. Pursue the same course with regard to painting, drawing and designing, and if you have power to obtain useful knowledge in any directions, do it. I have

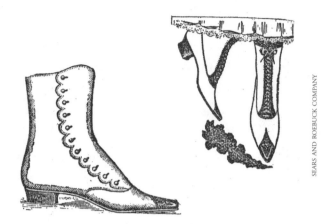

Dainty lace-up and button shoes peeked demurely from under long skirts. Heartier boots would have been worn for the long trek by covered wagon.

heard young men in speaking of their lady acquaintances say, "Oh, they look well, but they don't know anything." There is no necessity for such a state of things; books are cheap and accessible. If you have to labor all day in a shop or store, still at odd intervals you can gather up an education and contend with greater difficulties than did Clay, Fillmore, Webster and others of the greatest men. If you go through life a flying butterfly, how will you be spoken of by-and-by?

—Sacramento Bee, *California, August 1882*

Women wore special headwear indoors such as night-caps, morning or breakfast caps, day caps, and dress caps, all considered proper for home use. Nightcaps were typically made of wool to keep the head warm while sleeping, and some were colored and topped off with a tassel. Day caps were made to show the back of the hair, which was usually pinned up into a bun. Dress caps were a part of semi-formal evening wear and were dainty pieces of material attached to the hair directly below the crown of the head.

A quality pair of shoes rounded out a lady's daily costume and could often accentuate the overall look. Black or brown ankle-high laced boots, with square toes and wide heels, were generally worn until they were replaced by high-heeled button boots with pointy toes, introduced in the late 1870s.

CHAPTER 7

ALL DRESSED UP

A LOOK TO DIE FOR

"Men here in Tombstone will be killing each other over that gorgeous young actress!" exclaimed Peter Crawley.

The tall and slender gambler, looking in his prime in his early thirties, chuckled derisively. Then he began dressing his full blown, black mustache with deft fingers.

Taggit, his outlaw companion, opened, "The toughest town in America is trembling tonight just wondering what this here Donna Drew will do to it."

Crawley directed his intense gaze to the lithograph that hung above the arched, middle entrance of the Bird Cage Theatre. The theatrical sheet loomed in the light of the coal-oil street lamp below it.

"She's too beautiful to be alive," Crawley murmured. "An ace in the world's beauty-deck!" Then he read aloud the message heralded by the twenty-foot canvas banner set in a gilded frame that dressed the adobe building above the lithograph:

"Grand Opening—The Bird Cage Theatre. This Momentous Day, December 26, 1881. Presenting the Donna

An elegant bustle and train and sumptuous fabric distinguished this woman's appearance.

Drew Players of New York in the Breath-Taking Drama 'The Westerner.'"

Gambler and outlaw stood seemingly enchanted as they studied again the exquisiteness of the colored reproductions of a girl with red-yellow silken hair the front sides of which is waved and pulled back from the top into a huge, amorphous knot at the crown of the head. Long ringlets fall from the nape of the neck over her alabaster skin.

The nondescript crowd at Sixth and Allen Street muttered a conglomerate symphony of praises, as cowpunchers, miners, outlaws and townsfolk alike, gazed wistfully at the pictorial display.

Aloof from the front rank of riff-raff crowding the theatre's triple arched door, town-ladies bedecked in simple and neat frocks of the bustle and foot-length design, stood by their men-folk of acknowledged respectability.

Lily Delmar was among the women entering the theatre. She stood in the entrance of the building and searched the sea of faces for Crawley. When she spotted him she smiled. Her eyes finally met his for a moment, but then he looked away in disgust. Lily made her way over to the gambler and tapped him hard on the shoulder.

"Don't even think about trying to meet up with Donna Drew, Pete," she warned. "You're going to marry a dance-hall gal." Crawley's mouth stretched into an evil smile.

"I'll never marry you," he told her. "You don't have half the style Miss Drew has."

Lily swallowed hard and tears welled up in her eyes. "Run along now, my dear," he instructed unemotionally. "I'm going to see the show."

"You're going to see a funeral!" the girl announced bitterly.

These bustled dresses with their matching jackets and feathered hats were called "visiting costumes" or "visiting toilettes."

Crawley chuckled. *"You'd kill me, Lily?" He asked.*

"I love you so much I could slit your throat!" she choked back.

Crawley pushed past her and headed on towards the theatre. Lily froze for a moment. Her blue eyes flared with anguish and anger. Suddenly, she reached for a gun resting in the cowboy's holster standing next to her. She pointed it at Crawley and pulled the hammer back.

A gunshot rang out.

When the smoke cleared Crawley was holding a gun he had drawn from his own holster. He was calm, and deliberate. His eyes gave nothing away. He watched Lily slump to the ground and relax in the limpness of death. He walked over to the corpse as other people crowded around. The gambler's eyes seemed to glisten with sadistic pleasure.

Bending down next to Lily's body, he ripped a large, copper necklace hanging around her neck off the chain and studied it for a quick moment. "I always thought this was ugly," he mumbled to no one in particular. "Like I said . . . not half the style."

—Daily Tumbleweed, *Tombstone, Arizona, September, 1878*

SHINY ACCESSORIES AND OTHER FINERIES

Deciding what jewelry or hairstyle was most fashionable in the mid-1850s, in the far western regions of the United States, was a matter of personal taste. Eastern styles dictated what was in vogue, but that information was slow to reach the remote areas of the frontier. Residents of the Wild West created their own look, and at times were severely criticized by travelers who had just arrived from New York and Virginia.

It seems that women from Colorado and all points West lack the eye for appropriate metals to be worn for decoration. What they do wear is garish, bold and many times void of even a hint of femininity.

—*Letter in the* Sacramento Bee *from a Boston resident visiting the Gold Country, February 9, 1865*

LEGENDARY TRENDSETTER

LILLIAN RUSSELL

It is pretty generally understood that the costumes worn by Lillian Russell are novelties and models of the American dressmaker's art . . . The styles have never been known until they came into grace on the perfect form of the "Divine Lillian."

—*THE SAN FRANCISCO CALL*, CALIFORNIA, 1894

With her voluptuous figure, high plumed hats, and bejeweled gowns, Lillian Russell was the talk of the fashion world in the Gay Nineties. Onstage, she dared to wear purple tights and calf-high dresses that showed her naked ankles. Offstage, she was a meticulous dresser, adorned in diamonds and lace taffeta outfits. She was considered to be the ideal female of her generation, representing all that was glamorous.

Brooches and stickpins were often used to adorn women's dresses and men's cravats.

Jewelry worn by day was different from that worn at night. Daytime jewelry was simple and restrained. Brooches were used to fasten the collar at the neckline and were rarely, if ever, worn off to one side. Watches were pendants worn on a long chain.

Lockets could be worn either on a chain or a ribbon. Earrings, if worn, were either small rings or pendants with a wire hook, not post earrings.

For evening, bracelets, necklaces, earrings, and tiaras made of every possible kind of precious gem were acceptable. Semiprecious stones, such as garnets, were also worn for evening. Pearls were popular and a favorite ornament for many young girls.

The most fashionable jewelry of the decade was classically styled and included Greek and Roman artifacts, or smart replicas of them. Cameos, in particular, were stylish and were set in bracelets, brooches, rings, necklaces, and even tiaras. The gold nuggets gathered from streams and mountainsides were worn as decoration in everything from necklaces and stickpins to belt buckles and watch fobs. The nugget jewelry was highly sought after by people on the East Coast.

A select few felt that makeup and jewelry of any kind

Many women in the nineteenth century had their ears pierced and wore delicate earring such as these.

detracted from a woman's physical appearance and suggested that the human female form was most beautiful when left as nature intended. Newspapers and magazine articles proclaimed that the secret to true beauty was not the "finery used to dress the frame"; rather, "beauty came by expanding on all that is good and true in human life."

> *No individual can be educated on this plan and not have an impressive and pleasing countenance. Of course there are differences of inheritance to begin with, but every person possesses to a certain degree the germs of capacity in this direction, and if improvement be sought and preserved with, the results will be most gratifying. The essentials then to beauty are, first, good health; second, pure morals, and third, a cultivated mind. To be anything in this world at all, and be it well, one must have health.*
>
> *A good sound physical development is the basis of every great work. No man suffering from indigestion can elaborate pure thought. Crime itself is often, if not always, the offspring of a diseased body.*
>
> *No orator, no matter how much he has cultivated his intellect and built his ideas on moral principles, can thoroughly arouse or impress his audience unless he have physical health. No lady, however much nature may have kindly lavished upon her charms, can lay any claim to beauty unless the cheeks are tinged and the eyes beam and sparkle.*
> —The Sacramento Bee, *California, June 10, 1886*

Women's hairstyles of the time mirrored the lines in their gowns. If a woman's skirts were drawn up on the sides, her hair was worn pulled up in the same manner.

Curls and small twists at the back of the head mirrored the decoration on the backs of their dresses. Wearers of side bustles pulled their hair up, over their ears, allowing the back of their hair to fall upon the shoulders in a lavish twisted braid or in curls.

By 1876 hair was worn close and high on the head, giving ladies a smaller, neater appearance. A few curls might be arranged to fall from the back of the head to the shoulders in the evening. Hair was scraped up into a bun in the 1880s, with small tendrils framing the forehead. By the 1890s, hair was again dressed back from the forehead, but was fuller and softer, with a twist or bun on top of the head.

SEARLS LIBRARY, NEVADA COUNTY

Day Style #1

Evening and daytime hairstyles were quite distinctive. Fashionable women would never be seen in the light of day with relaxed curls, but tight up-dos could be worn at any time.

Day Style #1: This style shows the hair is waved and parted in the center, where it is pulled down behind the ears. A large chignon made of braids covers both the crown and the nape of her head.

Day Style #2: The hair is parted at the center front and drawn back behind the ears. Lots of hair product was needed to

Day Style #2

Evening Style #1

achieve this overly smooth look. A huge chignon that features twists of hair, braided together, circles over the top and back of the head.

Evening Style #1: The front and sides of the hair are pulled up toward the crown, and arranged in a large knot. The back hair is arranged into long ringlets.

Evening Style #2: The front of the hair is parted in the center, then pulled back over the ears toward the back of the head. It is allowed to stay very puffy over the ears. From the crown of the head, the hair is arranged into long twists that hang down to the nape of the neck and back up to the crown. At the crown, she wears ribbons and flowers that dangle to her shoulders.

Evening Style #3: This woman's hair includes more lift at the crown and drape at the neck. All of the hair is curled, the top pulled up toward the crown and arranged in an intricate array of knots. The back is a large roll or chignon that drapes onto the neck. Short, curled bangs are worn in front.

Between 1865 and 1890, men's hair was worn short with side and middle parts. The parts extended all the way from the front of the head to the nape of the neck during the 1870s, and to the crown only during the 1880s. Moustaches were frequently worn with beards during the 1880s, but a long, drooping moustache sans beard was also popular at the time. Clean-shaven faces made a comeback in 1889.

Both men and women seldom washed their hair. The natural oils from the head made the hair appear sleek and

Evening Style #2

Evening Style #3

shiny, a look that was considered quite fashionable at the time. Many ladies added more oil to their hair to dress it. It was removed at night by rubbing it with a cloth. Women brushed their hair repeatedly before going to bed to distribute the oil from the top of the head evenly to the ends of the strands.

CHAPTER 8

UNDER THE CLOTHES

ESSENTIALS IN INTIMATE APPAREL

Young ladies today are insufficiently clad, both for propriety in evening dress and for health in the day. Physicians attribute the habit of "catching colds" to draughts and imperfect closure of windows, especially in the bedroom. Our fair country women fear water; this, with insufficient clothing (a practice arising from the silly vanity of appearing small-waisted) are the true causes. The undergarments worn "at least over her vital organs," are totally inadequate, and bare shoulders in an evening dress is largely instrumental in starting consumptions. The chest should be carefully guarded but the garments should be porous, and for that reason leather waist coats and rabbit skins should be avoided. Flannel should be worn next to the skin all the year over the whole body and arms and as low as the middle of the thighs, but alas! Very few young ladies will do so. Ladies should not be sparing of flannel petticoats, and drawers are an incalculable advantage to women, preventing many of the disorders and indispositions to which females are subject.

—The Handbook of the Toilet, *1841*

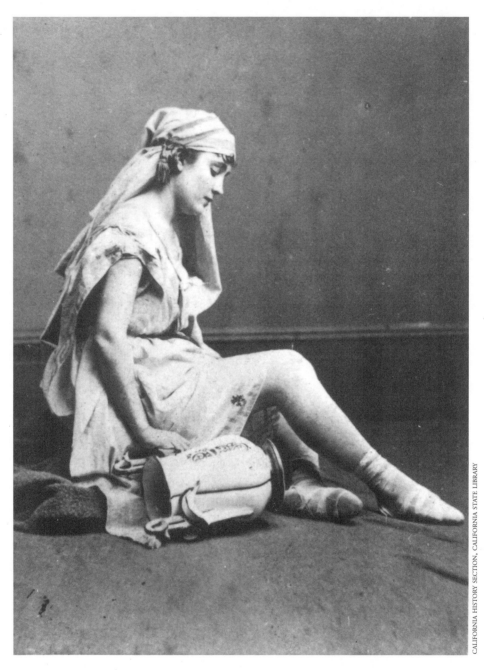

Adah Menken's on-stage personae inspired women to challenge fashion trends.

UNDERWEAR FOR MEN, WOMEN, AND CHILDREN

On August 24, 1863, San Francisco's elite flocked to Maguire's Opera House. Ladies wearing diamonds and furs rode up in handsome carriages; gentlemen in opera capes and silk hats were also in attendance. It was an opening night such as the city had never before seen. All 1,000 seats in the theater were filled with curious spectators, anxious to see the celebrated melodramatic actress Adah Menken perform.

Adah was starring in the role that made her famous—that of Prince Ivan in *Mazeppa*. It was rumored that she preferred to play the part in the nude. Newspapers in the East reported that the audiences found the scantily clad thespian's act "shocking, scandalous, horrifying and even delightful."

The storyline of the play was taken from a Byron poem, in which a Tartar prince is condemned to ride forever in the desert, stripped naked and lashed to a fiery, untamed steed. Adah insisted on playing the part as true to life as possible.

The audience waited with bated breath for Adah to walk out on stage, and when she did, a hush fell over the crowd. She was beautiful, with dark hair and large, dark eyes. Adorned in a flesh-colored body nylon and tight-fitting underwear, she left the audience speechless.

During the play's climactic scene, supporting characters strapped the star to the back of a black stallion. The horse raced up a narrow runway between cardboard representatives of mountain crags. The audience responded with thunderous applause. Adah Menken and her revealing undergarments left the ticket holders in a state of shock—and scandalized the West.

Bold women like Adah Menken who dared to break

*Elaborate lace-trimmed
undergarments and nightgowns
were considered essential to the
wardrobe of wealthy and middle-
class women of the late 1800s.*

fashion traditions paved the way for a less confining order of dress for ladies throughout the frontier. Victorian women rarely, if ever, spoke of intimate garments. Considered too improper an item to even make by hand, undergarments were acquired solely through newspaper, magazine, and catalog advertisements.

Corsets were one of the most popular mail-order unmentionables. In the never-ending quest to reveal a figure under yards of material in skirts, blouses, and capes, women wore the close-fitting cincher to highlight their waist and hips. Corsets were of lightweight material and constructed with whalebone, or wooden or metal pieces to stiffen the fabric. They were designed to constrict the waist and lift the bust while creating a smooth line under a tight-fitting bodice. Members of the medical profession—particularly female physicians on staff at the women's medical college in Philadelphia—declared such constraints on the form "an enemy to female health." Churches, too, proclaimed that "tight lacing" morally opposed the laws of religion.

Contrary to the stories that have circulated for centuries, a properly fitted corset did not prohibit breathing, and women did not have lower ribs removed to permit tighter lacing of corset ties. There were some women who tried to squeeze their waists beyond the standard 2 inches usually provided by the corset. Those ladies generally suffered for their fashion.

*A belle of the ball in San Antonio purchased a new silk dress
that fit so tightly she had to wear a corset for the first time*

in her life. She was several times compelled to escape to her bedroom to take off the corset and "catch her breath."
—*Pioneer Mary Maverick, 1841*

Underpants, or pantalets, were believed to prevent disease and infection. They were generally made of flannel, angora, calico, or cotton, and the legs extended to just above the ankle. In the winter months, lamb's wool underwear was worn.

A loose shirt-like undergarment, known as a chemise, was worn over the underpants. The chemise came with either short or long gathered sleeves, and was trimmed in lace from the drawstring neck to the hem. It was worn more for modesty's sake than as protection from the elements. Also available was a combination drawers-and-chemise outfit known as a "union suit."

The brassiere, as it is now called, was once referred to as a "bust improver." According to the *Handbook of the Toilet,* the device was made of an air-proof material and promised that its user would get a "sylph-like roundness to the waist without restraint or pressure." An 1855 Sears, Roebuck and Company advertisement assured ladies that the "bust improver" would "add a fullness to their dress."

Bustles also added a fullness to a woman's dress, sometimes in the back and later on the sides. This "dress improver," as it was more commonly called in 1849, provided the skirt with a domed shape. It was replaced by the crinoline in 1856.

The last item on every woman's list of undergarments was stockings. These extended above the wearer's knees and were held in place by a leather of silk garter. In 1860 stockings

The corset was worn by women to achieve a desirable hourglass figure, but its use was decried by most knowledgeable medical practitioners and some clergymen.

A chemise was worn under a dress or blouse in summer, while heavier long underwear might be worn in winter.

LEGENDARY TRENDSETTER

ANDREW JOHNSON

Before he became the President of the United States, Andrew Johnson was a tailor of renowned reputation. He began his career as an apprentice to a tailor in Raleigh, North Carolina. During his twelve-hour workday, he became an expert fabric cutter and tailor. In 1827 he opened his own shop and created a popular variation on the Prince Albert–style coat. The double-breasted, knee-length coat was reproduced by other tailors and worn by politicians and wealthy businessmen heading to San Francisco during the height of the Gold Rush. Johnson charged $8.00 for each coat, but following the custom of the time, he often bartered with his clients, accepting flour, beef, wood, and other goods as a form of payment.

came primarily in two colors, black and magenta. By the early 1880s stockings were offered in a variety of different colors, including yellow.

An under-vest was to a man what a chemise was to a woman. Often made of flannel, it was worn for extra warmth and helped protect the skin from outer garments. A gentleman's drawers were ankle-length garments made from silk stockinet. The front 9-inch opening was covered by a 2-inch over-flap in the waistband and held together with buttons. A 4-inch opening down the center of the back stayed fastened with silk tape. A pair of elastic braces held both the underpants and the trousers up.

Most people washed before dressing but did not have an indoor bathroom. The frontier version of a bath consisted of filling a washtub with water, which had first been heated on a fire, and then immersing oneself—usually in the comfort of the family kitchen. The task was time-consuming and uncomfortable, and those factors made bathing a rarity. Once-a-week baths were considered the norm. For the remainder of the week, sponge baths were preferred. Women who had blemishes were advised by pioneer doctors to use soap on their faces daily during each sponge bath. Physicians considered this the best remedy for a clear complexion and soft cheeks and hands.

Those concerned about taking care of their health do not need medicine. Many women are much troubled by little black speckles about the mouth and nose called "black heads." Some ascribe to them the romanticism of ill health.

I regret to say that it is simple dirt—the result of mining

Knee-length bloomers were worn under skirts in summer.

A woolen Union suit was worn for warmth in winter.

Store-bought fancy soaps were a treat for middle- and upper-class nineteenth-century men and women.

soot and winds impregnated by black soil. The best way to get rid of them is to make a stiff soapy lather and use hot water, hot as you can bear it.

—Doctor Herbert Cantrall, Riverside Enterprise Medical Journal, *California, July 1892*

According to many medical journals of the time, early American doctors maintained that much, if not all, of a woman's complexion problems could be blamed upon cosmetics. It was considered improper for "decent single ladies" to wear makeup, but married women sometimes used flesh colored powders and lip balms with a faint rose hue. Journals kept by pioneer women indicate that both single and married women would pinch their cheeks to give them a pinkish glow.

We cannot but allude to the practice of using paints, a habit strongly condemned. If for no other reason than that poison lurks beneath every layer, inducing paralytic affections and premature death, they should be discarded—but they are a disguise which deceives no one, even at a distance; there is a ghastly deathliness in the appearance of the skin after it has been painted, which is far removed from the natural hue of health.

—Frank Leslie's Illustrated Newspaper, 1878

In spite of these opinions, many women did accentuate their looks with homemade cosmetics. Candle soot was used as eyeliner, and the petals from certain flowers was used to make lips and cheeks pink. Women preferred makeup that gave them a pearl finish. Garish, bold makeup and a greasy face were looked upon as being just as unattractive as a suntan. Women kept their faces and shoulders carefully shaded from the sun to prevent freckles and tanning. Those who were exposed to the strong rays often tried to remedy the situation by bleaching their skin with lemon juice. Newspapers across the West frequently devoted entire columns to the browning of white skin and offered advice on how to reverse the look.

The summer's cost of tan if not removed from day to day by the use of proper cosmetic lotions is likely to be a source of much annoyance to the woman who has been having a good time away from home. When she gets back, she consults her friends and her own memory for remedies to remove the tan, and she usually in despair ends letting it remain on her face. It is ever easy to acquire the tan, but difficult to remove it.

The best way would have been to take precautions early in the season, but since it is on, use a good cold cream every night on retiring, and when the face is washed put a little skin lotion in the water with which it is bathed. When going out in the sun a pure powder should be applied to the skin in order that the skin may not become leathery.

When coming in from walking, if you feel warm, do not wash the face, rub a little cold cream into the pores and let it remain for a while.

There is no way to remove this tan at once, but wait with patience until the cold cream and the lotion have done their work. Skin bleaches are dangerous, for nearly all contain mercury or some harmful drug, which in sufficiently large quantities, is poisonous to the skin. The better way to remove the tan is to consult a good skin specialist who prepares lotions for that purpose, as the summer rays of the sun often times bring discolorations that simple remedies will not

Men's undergarments were typically as modest as women's and were usually worn year-round.

Knee-high stockings might be held up with a garter or the bottom of lacy drawers.

remove. The summer girl must not neglect her complexion,
as exposure to the air ages the skin.

—The Denver Republican,
Colorado, September 1899

Along with homemade cosmetics, women often complemented their appearance with perfumes. Perfumes covered odors that might arise from the lack of daily bathing. Women mixed cloves, nutmeg, Tonga beans, and orris root together to produce a distinctive scent. The concoction was then poured into a sachet bag and sewn into corsets.

CHAPTER 9

STYLE IN THE RANKS

HAT IN HAND

A battle-weary Lieutenant James Bennett led his troop of equally tired and tried men through the wooden gates at Fort Thorn, New Mexico. The anxious eyes of the residents at the Fort watched the soldiers drag themselves off their rides and nearly collapse from exhaustion. Several of the troops were injured—the arrows shot from the bows of the Mescalero Apaches still embedded in their arms and legs. Wives and dependents of the wounded regiment members hurried out to assist their loved ones to the post hospital.

Mrs. Ira Stanton stood on the porch of her quarters scanning the faces of the soldiers, hoping to see her husband, Captain Henry Whiting Stanton. Unable to find him she walked out to speak with the Lieutenant. Her voice was calm as she began to speak. "Is the Captain coming along with the others?" she asked. "There are no others," the Lieutenant gently replied. Her eyes searched his face for the answer to her next hopeless question. He turned away from her only for a moment and retrieved an item from his saddlebag. Handing the desperate Mrs. Stanton the Captain's forage cap he said, "He died trying to save us all." Iris held her deceased husband's dark blue,

Soldiers in forage caps mingle with civilians at the Good Old Days Canteen in Fort Keough, Montana, c. 1890.

Army issued hat tightly in her hand and tears stained her cheeks.

"Poor woman," the Lieutenant later wrote in his report of the widow Stanton. "Him she loved, she shall never more behold. She is left with only pieces of his uniform to remember him by."

—The Evening Citizen, *Albuquerque, New Mexico, June 1875*

CLOTHING OF THE WESTERN SOLDIER

Members of the United States Dragoons, like Captain Henry Stanton, were provided with all of their clothing—from hats to boots. The manner of dress for military men in the West was not consistent from post to post. Uniforms were similar in

Soldiers in hot, wool uniforms and forage caps train at Fort Baynard, New Mexico Territory in 1891.

style but not identical. The shades of blue varied greatly, and more often than not, the government-issued attire for enlisted men did not fit well. Some had their clothing altered to fit better, but most did not. Officers, on the other hand, were not provided with uniforms. They were given a clothing allowance, with which they purchased their own gear, often investing in quality tailor-made material and embellishing on the regulated style.

Soldiers stationed at rough outposts like Fort Thorn had only one issue of everyday fatigues and one dress uniform. Additional clothing was secured from fellow soldiers who had died in battle. An infantryman's hat was one of the few items that was generally not passed along to another recruit.

In 1870 there were thirty-two active military posts in the West, with no more than 250 men assigned to a post. A daily outfit for the average soldier consisted of a dark blue, single-

The ladies, gentlemen, and children of Fort Bridger, in what is now Wyoming, gather for a photograph in 1873.

breasted wool shirt, or a white or gray flannel shirt, and light blue wool trousers worn with a belt or suspenders over long-handled underwear. Until 1858 pant legs were worn over basic black boots, which had wooden soles and heels. The standard cavalry boot was 14 inches high. Infantrymen wore lace-up shoes called booties.

Infantrymen also wore a black felt hat with a 6½-inch high, flat-topped crown. Both sides of the brim were pinned up with an eagle insignia. Enlisted men wore dark blue wool forage caps with tarred-leather visors and no insignia with both dress uniforms and fatigues. Soldiers who had survived a military conflict but had suffered a loss of limb often pinned their uniforms with bugle insignias.

Whether it was related to an injury or simply for survival, soldiers altered their uniforms to fit their changing needs. During the frigid winter months on the frontier, soldiers kept

warm by wearing several layers of their uniforms over flannel underwear. The army issued each frontier soldier a sack coat, or fatigue jacket, to provide protection from the cold, but they were often abandoned in favor of non-regulation coats made of buffalo or bear hide. A heavy outer garment called a "great coat" was worn over an officer's uniform. The great coats were made from a stockpile of government cloth left over from the Civil War. Later, blanket-lined coats were provided for men of all ranks. Winter wear for officers consisted of dark blue, single-breasted frock coats over light blue wool pants, which had a 1½-inch-wide stripe running down the leg seam. Infantry and cavalry soldiers' uniforms had different colored stripes.

During the 1860s cavalrymen wore their pants tucked into their boots for additional warmth and protection from the elements. At times soldiers would also wrap their boots in burlap sacks to keep their feet from freezing.

Winter conditions meant bundling up on horseback. These scouts returning from Wounded Knee, c. 1890, were barely recognizable on their mounts.

LEGENDARY TRENDSETTERS

GEORGE AND ELIZABETH CUSTER

Clothing historians believe that no couple made more of an impact on western fashion than George and Elizabeth Custer. George, the "Boy General," carried on his duties as commander of the Seventh Cavalry dressed in fringed, buckskin breeches and a jacket, a navy-blue shirt with a wide falling collar and a red cravat. His men so admired the look that they adopted it for the entire regiment. Custer's sense of style extended to women's clothing as well. Elizabeth accompanied her husband on field maneuvers dressed in hoop skirts that measured five yards around the bottom. But at times, the prairie wind would blow the skirt up and expose her petticoat. So George designed an outfit for his wife that included a military-style riding jacket, a pleated under-shirt, and a less cumbersome skirt. Strips of lead were sewn into the dress hems to keep it weighted down in a strong breeze.

LITTLE BIGHORN BATTLEFIELD

In 1872 the United States Army redesigned its basic uniform, giving it a more "regal look." Artillery privates' dress blues now included scarlet trim cording, tassels, and helmets with horsehair plumes. With this change, the military hoped to attract a better class of recruits and renew pride in their seasoned veterans. A new five-button fatigue blouse of dark blue flannel with a high collar was issued, along with sky-blue jersey trousers, the sides of which were reinforced with canvas. Folding campaign caps, made of black felt and with wide, oval-shaped brims to provide shade, were now the norm. White dress gloves made of a cotton and wool blend were worn for all special events and post inspections.

I have seen various kinds of soldiers, and I ran up to the state camp at Peekskill when the famous 7th Regiment was in camp, in the expectation of seeing yet another kind. In this I was disappointed, for whatever the men of the 7th may be in citizens' clothes, they are much like other men in the new Army uniform. I do not mean in their full dress uniform; in that they are like the lilies of the field in their gorgeousness, but I must say, and it is a heresy which will damn one, that the full dress is more capable of destroying all semblance of the Creator's image than anything except a bishop's robe or a butcher's linen.

—The journal of Frederick Remington, 1872

The American frontier soldier's uniform also included his weapons and other supplies. Soldiers carried bedding, sabers, mess kits, canteens, bayonets, rifles, and cartridge boxes with ammunition. Sabers were primarily used as decoration—they were not carried into battle because they made an undue

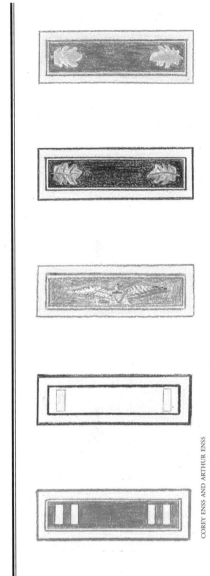

COREY ENSS AND ARTHUR ENSS

Chevrons and other insignia indicated at first glance the rank and position of a soldier. From top to bottom, these were worn by a major in the artillery, a lieutenant colonel, a colonel in the infantry, a first lieutenant in the cavalry, and a captain in the infantry.

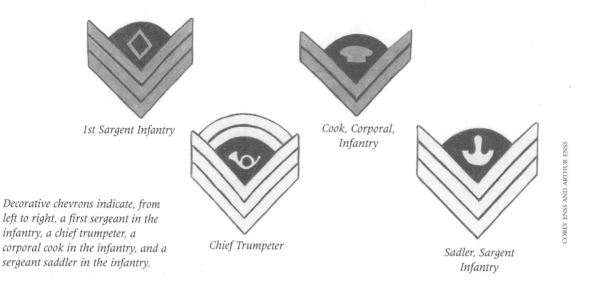

1st Sargent Infantry

Cook, Corporal, Infantry

Decorative chevrons indicate, from left to right, a first sergeant in the infantry, a chief trumpeter, a corporal cook in the infantry, and a sergeant saddler in the infantry.

Chief Trumpeter

Sadler, Sargent Infantry

A lieutenant general, a major general, and a brigadier general, distinguished by their stars.

amount of noise and were a hindrance to free movement. The .50 caliber, single-shot Spencer carbine was also considered cumbersome for foot soldiers to carry and was a secondary weapon to the .44 caliber Colt sidearm.

According to newspaper accounts of the 1870s, military experts differed over which were the most effective weapons a soldier should take into battle, and how they should handle their firearms. Soldiers submitted letters of support for their favorite weapon to commanding officers, in hopes that they would become standard issue.

Every man who goes into Indian country should be armed with a rifle and a revolver, and he should never, either in camp or out of it, lose sight of them. When not on a march, they should be placed in such a position that they can be seized at an instant's warning; and when moving about outside the camp, the revolver should invariably be worn in the belt, as the person does not know at what moment he may have use for it.

My own experience has forced me to the conclusion that

the breech-loading arm possesses great advantages over the muzzle-loading, for the reason that it can be charged and fired with much greater rapidity.

Colt's revolving pistol is the most efficient arm of its kind. It gives six shots in more rapid succession than any other rifle I know of. I cannot resist the force of my conviction that, if I were alone upon the prairies, and expected an attack from a body of Indians, I am not acquainted with any arm I would as soon have in my hands as this.

—Artillery Sergeant Daniel Barnett, Ellsworth, Kansas, September 14, 1877

The type of weapon a soldier carried was indicative of the man's rank or position in the service. Chevrons, an insignia consisting of stripes meeting at an angle and worn on the sleeve of a uniform, denoted rank as well. The chevrons on an officer's "cloak coat" were indicated on both sleeves by silk braids. The chevron for an infantryman, or field soldier, had a bugle emblem affixed in the center. Chevrons were to be worn with the points down and above the elbow, on both overcoats and dress coats.

Civilians who dreamed of wearing a uniform with the insignia of their choice had to meet certain qualifications before enlisting. Potential soldiers had to be able-bodied and of good character. They could weigh no more than 150

Some aspects of formality were abandoned by soldiers in the field. Uniforms became whatever was comfortable and practical to wear under the circumstances.

pounds, stand between five foot five and five foot ten, and be between the ages of eighteen and thirty-five. Horsemanship was not a requisite. Hair and beards had to be kept short and neatly trimmed. A $100 bonus was paid to any man who enlisted for three years; he would earn an average of $13 a month.

CHAPTER 10

BORROWED FROM THE LAND

THE SAVOIR-FAIRE OF SITTING BULL

I do not know for certain whether I met Sitting Bull, the great Sioux Indian warrior, in 1876 or not. He was not at the time a chief of any note; in fact, he was not much of a chief but more of a medicine man. It was General Sheridan who really made him a "big Indian." They had to have some name for that war, and I was on the mission at Red Cloud Agency when they were talking about what name to give it. They spoke of Chief Gall, Crazy Horse, and others, all bigger men than Sitting Bull's war, and that made him seem to be a great man, and his name became known all over the country.

The first time I ever saw him to know him was when he joined my show at Buffalo, coming with eight or nine of his chosen people from Grand River. They wore their ghost shirts made of cotton cloth, painted blue around the necks, with designs of great originality: stars shaped like peyote birds; stars in the shape of Maltese crosses; bright-colored thunder-birds; bows and arrows and suns and moons. Sitting Bull appeared before 10,000 people, and was hissed, so it was some time before I could talk to the crowd and secure their

Either Babeshikit, a Kickapoo, poses in garb that combines native tradition and western influence.

patience. The same thing occurred at almost every place. He never did more than appear on horseback at any performance, and always refused to talk English, even if he could.

At Philadelphia, a man asked him if he had no regret at killing Custer and so many whites. He replied, "I have answered to my people for the Indians slain in that fight. The chief that sent Custer must answer to his people." That is the only smart thing I ever heard him say.

—William "Buffalo Bill" Cody, 1879

CLOTHING OF THE NATIVE AMERICANS

Hundreds of thousands of Native Americans occupied the West at one time. Some lived in tepees made of brush and skin, while others occupied cliff dwellings dotting the sides of hills. Each cultural group had a distinctive way of living, working, and dressing. From the Plains to the Pacific Northwest, traditional styles within tribes reflected their spirit and rich heritage.

Plains Indians, those tribes residing in a broad area from the Mississippi to the Rocky Mountains, wore garments made from buffalo and deer hide and decorated with beads. Porcupine quills and feathers were then added to the garment. The patterns and designs that were used symbolized the wearer's wealth and social status.

Men wore breechcloths—deerskin pants stretched between the legs and held in place with a leather belt. Women wore loose-fitted, long-sleeved dresses, stitched together with deerskin and decorated with fringe, beads, and small pieces of metal. Ceremonial clothing items were painted in vibrant reds and blues, and adorned with shells and quillwork. In cold weather both men and women wore buffalo robes and boots. Easterners who saw pioneer sketches of this warm look quickly went to work to make it their own.

Ninety-six thousand Buffalo robes have been imported since the beginning of the spring, into New York. These warm and popular coverings are invariably tanned by the women Indians, the brutal braves considering such work unworthy of them.

—Frank Leslie's Illustrated Newspaper, *October 13, 1860*

This etching depicts Pehriska-Ruhpa of the Dog Band of the Hidatsa in full ceremonial regalia.

The sight of Native Americans on the frontier left a lasting impression on many wide-eyed pioneers. Some military dependents, stationed with their loved ones in outposts across the West, found Indians decked out in headdresses and buffalo robes to be fearless and frightening, as well as daring and handsome.

Just about sunset, "Standing Elk"—a fine specimen of the Brule Sioux, and who, in company with "Spotted Tail," "Two Strike," and "Swift Bear," again visited us at Fort

A Hopi man has his hair dressed, probably by his wife.

McPherson in 1867. Standing Elk and his companions were dressed in part in their native wardrobe and the white man's. They wore feathered headdresses decorated with tufts of red-dyed horse hair. Blankets were draped around buckskin pants and colorful shirts and vests. These men had come to pay their respects, receive a payment of tobacco, and have a talk. Standing Elk asked us where we were going, and was frankly told the destination of the command. He then told us that "a treaty was being talked about at Laramie with a great many Indians, some of whom belonged in the country to which we were going; but that the fighting men of those

HOW THE WEST WAS WORN

bands had not come in, and would not; but that we would have to fight them, as they would not sell their hunting grounds to the white men for a road."

He exhibited all indications of sincere friendship, and said that he and Spotted Tail would sign the treaty and would always be "friends." They were magnificent to look upon.

—Army wife Margaret Irvin Carrington, 1868

The Plateau Indians lived in the northern part of eastern Oregon. The climate there was very harsh. Summers were extremely hot, and winters were long and very cold. Some of the tribes that lived in this area were the Nez Perce, Cayuse, Umatilla, and Tygh.

Hairstyles might identify the tribe—in this case the Chief of the Little Osage shows a proud profile.

Indians of the plateau moved in a cycle. At different times of the year, they traveled to food-gathering places, hunting grounds, and fishing spots. The people of the plateau area wore robes and dresses made from the skins of deer, mountain goats, bighorn sheep, and occasionally of woven bark fibers. Leggings and moccasins made of animal skin were also worn.

California Indians wore apparel made from bear, rabbit, and deer hides. According to *American West* magazine, it took 100 rabbits to make one coat for winter. Native Americans in the Northwest wore clothing made primarily of animal products such as seal, Arctic fox, bear, and other furs. Some garments were even made from tree bark.

LEGENDARY TRENDSETTER

BUFFALO BILL CODY

Buffalo Bill is a magnificent specimen of a man, and has a native grace of movement that is quite captivating. And a look that is unique and fitting to his work.

—*THE CHICAGO REVIEW*, 1872

William Frederick Cody was a frontiersman and noted marksman of the American West. Not only did he bring Wild West shows into prominence, he was a bit of a fashion plate, as well. His knee-length fringe shirts, ornamental leather coats, engraved and embroidered thigh-high boots, and broad-brimmed hat made him one of the most recognizable figures in the United States and Europe. His curly, shoulder-length hair, thin moustache, and small goatee accentuated the look. Costume historians credit Buffalo Bill with "bringing a bit of sophistication to the unruly plains."

Southwest Native Americans dressed to protect themselves from cactus plants, harmful snakes and insects, and the heat. Throughout the eighteenth century, long leather leggings were worn by both men and women year-round, to protect them from the rough terrain and its fierce inhabitants. Other garments were made from cloth that kept the wearer comfortable in blistering temperatures. When the heat became too oppressive, men and boys would go without shirts.

An Indian's footwear was considered one of the most important parts of his dress. Each tribe had its own moccasin shape and decoration. The moccasins of Plains Indians had hard, thick soles, giving them greater protection from thorny brush and hard prairie ground. The moccasins of Woodland Indians, on the other hand, had a softer sole, as the ground covering in their region predominantly consisted of pine needles and thick, heavy grass. During cold winters and heavy wet snow, moccasins of another type had to be used. These were waterproofed to some degree by making soles and uppers from the well-smoked skin tops of old lodges. Although not perfectly waterproofed, these could withstand months of trekking across wet ground without becoming hard or cracked. These cold-weather moccasins also had high

Six Zuni men wear traditional clothing with leather boots.

San Juan, a Mescalero Apache chief, is photographed in ceremonial dress.

NATIONAL ARCHIVES, WESTERN COLLECTION

buckskin tops to protect the ankles, with long leather thongs as fasteners. Since they were designed purely for hard service, there was no need to decorate this type of footwear. To keep the feet warm and comfortable, leaves, sagebrush bark, and clipped buffalo hair was matted to make insulation pads of various thicknesses.

Winter moccasins were either made with animal hair turned inward, or they were cut extra large so that heavy inner wrappings could be added. Moccasins intended for ceremonial and festival use had decorations covering the entire upper portion and tongues. Older styles were colorfully decorated with animal quills.

Southern Cheyenne moccasins had broad scallop designs, while the Sioux often had tops that were quilled in long red and green triangles, with beads in white, red, blue, and yellow, stepped edges. Beaded moccasins of the Crows had a U-shaped beaded area on top, or green and red designs interweaving across the top. Both Comanche and Kiowa footwear had a pointed toe shaped with strong diagonal lines in the beading.

Their copper-skinned faces were wrinkled from long years beneath the sun. They were serious and thoughtful. They wore soft buckskin, skirts, leggings, and moccasins—fringed and beaded here and there or hung with shells and bits of tinkling metal. They wore silver pendants on leather thongs or neck-

HOW THE WEST WAS WORN

*laces of shells, beads, or bear's claw or elk's teeth. And on
their braided hair were wrappings of fur or tanned skin. On
their feet decorated moccasins women in the East would long
to have.*

*—Pioneer Grace Linton on her first encounter with
members of the Cheyenne tribe, 1875*

Native Americans were devoted to land, tribe, and tradition, and their respect for these aspects of their lives were reflected in their wardrobe. Unlike the invaders of their world, their manner of dress had meaning. The color of their garments symbolized the moon and sun, earth and sky. Some Native Americans associated the length of their hair with physical stamina and moral strength. Drawings of a warrior's hunting trips or heroics in battled were painted on their buckskin aprons and often featured their long hair prominently as part of the design. Native Americans' distinct style was designed to be in harmony with the land. From their elaborate headdresses to their deer-hide moccasins, their unique manner of dress struck fear in the hearts of naïve settlers, while prompting trappers and fur traders to duplicate it.

SUGGESTED READING

Dunnington, Tom. *Hats Are for Watering Horses.* Chicago: Rand McNally and Company, 1975.

Hall, Lee. *Common Threads: A Parade of American Clothing.* Canada: Bullfinch Press, 1992.

Hansen, Henny H. *Costumes and Styles.* Chicago: E.D. Dutton Company, 1974.

Irwin, John. *The Kashmir Shawl.* Canada: Victoria and Albert Museum Press, 1973.

Kalman, Bobbie. *Historic Communities.* New York: Crabtree Publishing, 1993.

Worrell, Estelle A. *Early American Costume.* Harrisburg, Penn.: Stackpole Books, 1975.

ABOUT THE AUTHOR

Chris Enss is an award-winning screenwriter who has written for television, short subject films, live performances, and for the movies, and is the co-author (with JoAnn Chartier) of *Love Untamed: True Romances Stories of the Old West, Gilded Girls: Women Entertainers of the Old West,* and *She Wore A Yellow Ribbon: Women Patriots and Soldiers of the Old West* and *The Cowboy and the Senorita* and *Happy Trails* (with Howard Kazanjian). Her research and writing and reveals the funny, touching, exciting, and tragic stories of historical and contemporary times.

Enss has done everything from stand-up comedy to working as a stunt person at the Old Tucson Movie Studio. She learned the basics of writing for film and television at the University of Arizona, and she is currently working with *Return of the Jedi* producer Howard Kazanjian on the movie version of *The Cowboy and the Senorita,* their biography of western stars Roy Rogers and Dale Evans.

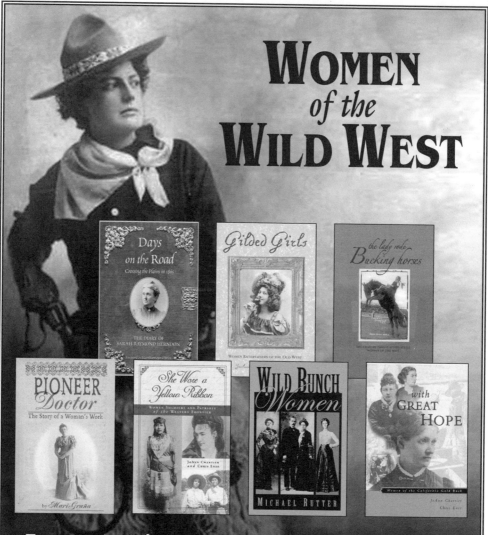